NINE FRIENDS

Maximizing Your Forum

Vince Corsaro

ISBN: 978-0-557-34426-0

NINE FRIENDS:
MAXIMIZING YOUR FORUM

All worksheets and other resources may be downloaded free of charge for personal forum use: www.theprincipalsforum.org. Additional copies and the most recent version of *"Nine Friends: Maximizing Your Forum"* may be purchased at www.amazon.com, or by contacting help@theprincipalsforum.org.

SECTION I: A CASE FOR NINE FRIENDS

"I have plenty of acquaintances but very few friends."
"I wish I had a place to take off all my masks."
"With work and family commitments, I've sacrificed taking care of me for now."

Is this you? With today's technology we are more connected than ever before in the history of the world. Why then do so many people report feeling isolated and alone? What is it that blocks us from engaging in authentic relationships? Why is it that we share pictures of dinner or post our favorite songs, yet avoid talking about the real issues, feelings of inadequacy, fears about the future, and our closest held hopes and dreams?

In *"Leaders Eat Last"*, Simon Sinek explores the chemical "reward" that comes with personal accomplishment. He shares that our bodies treat even a "like" on a social media site as an accomplishment and give us a small "hit" of the hormones that make us feel good. And, we've become addicted to this short-burst fix! In many ways, we've traded the long-term feelings of connection and bonding with others for the quick hit, adrenaline rush, the "wow". The consequences are more stress, more fear of missing out, and less true connection.

Most behaviorists and thought leaders in the field of personal growth agree that we need voices in our lives that draw out our strengths and help support our areas of weakness. We need people who hold the mirror up to us and let us know what they see. From their observations, we gain a deeper understanding of how we are wired. We connect to ourselves as we allow ourselves to connect to others.

The bottom line: We need friends. We are wired to connect and live in community. That's no surprise. But, how do we do it in a 24/7 world?

About Forum

Many leaders who care deeply about their impact often report a sense of isolation once they have moved into a senior leadership role. They are consumed with their daily challenges, setting the right tone, and often unsure they are implementing best practices. They desire a safe and respectful place where they can connect with others in similar roles and air out the issues they face. While the formal structure in which leaders work often provides some support for the tactical issues of their jobs, there is little opportunity to holistically explore their unique situation. Forum provides a solution to these needs.

Call it a "circle", a "kitchen cabinet", or even a "tribe" and you'll get to about the same place: a small group of peers, committed to engaging together through the rough and tumble realities of life. As such, forum becomes a perfect expression of community and is used by leaders and business professionals throughout the world. Several international organizations use forum as a cornerstone of the membership experience, including YPO, The Principals' Forum, Executive Roundtable, The Entrepreneurs' Organization, and others.

In practice, most forums meet monthly for 3-4 hours in a prescribed format. Each meeting gives members an opportunity to share, in a confidential and safe environment, their challenges, aspirations and frustrations. In doing so, they learn from the similar shared experiences of other members and best practices for solving dilemmas, refocusing towards the lessons of leadership and personal growth they have learned in the past.

From Forum Members:

"Thank you, again for the opportunity to network with colleagues in such a professional-yet casual manner. I believe we all left the room a little wiser than when we walked in."

~~~~

"I thought you were going to make us sing Kum-Ba-Yah! And, there was a part of me that wanted to."

~~~~

"Forum has given me a place to explore my immaturities as I strive to live in my maturity."

Forums may also gather for various educational or social events as desired. Successful forums agree on a unified vision, ground rules for behavior, and expectations for shared responsibilities. Each forum creates a unique identity recognizing the strengths, weaknesses, and capacities of each member. Leadership is shared. Care and affection take place spontaneously as the line between work and play is blurred and both are enjoyed at once.

All people belong to multiple communities and groups: extended families, work teams, faith congregations, sports teams, neighborhoods, towns, cities, and countries. Most people have professional support networks that include bankers, lawyers, accountants, financial advisors, and many others. And, most people have a fabric of personal relationships including loved ones, longtime associates, and informal friends. Forum stands alone as a unique and special place to bring the issues in life that cross all boundaries and do not have a home elsewhere - the highest highs and the lowest lows.

At their best, forum relationships achieve high levels of authenticity, where what is going on inside each member is matched by what is coming out on the outside! Author M. Scott Peck describes this as a journey from "pseudo" or "nicey-nice" relationships to one that says, "I want to be in authentic relationship with you."

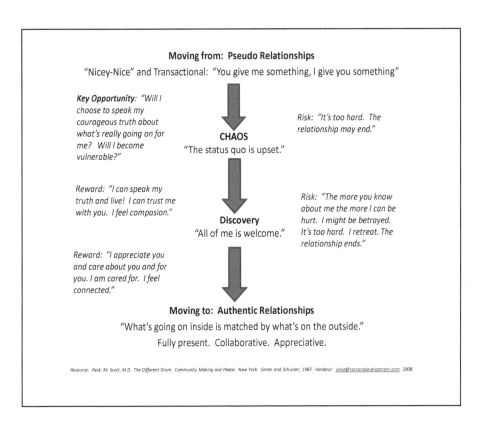

Moving from: Pseudo Relationships
"Nicey-Nice" and Transactional: "You give me something, I give you something"

Key Opportunity: "Will I choose to speak my courageous truth about what's really going on for me? Will I become vulnerable?"

Risk: "It's too hard. The relationship may end."

CHAOS
"The status quo is upset."

Reward: "I can speak my truth and live! I can trust me with you. I feel compasion."

Risk: "The more you know about me the more I can be hurt. I might be betrayed. It's too hard. I retreat. The relationship ends."

Discovery
"All of me is welcome."

Reward: "I appreciate you and care about you and for you. I am cared for. I feel connected."

Moving to: Authentic Relationships
"What's going on inside is matched by what's on the outside."
Fully present. Collaborative. Appreciative.

Resource: Peck, M. Scott, M.D. The Different Drum: Community Making and Peace. New York: Simon and Schuster, 1987. Handout: vince@corsarodevelopment.com 2008.

The target is to create a forum experience where each member takes 100% responsibility for their involvement, emotions and thoughts are un-masked, appreciation is genuine, with creativity and collaboration flowing freely in an environment of curiosity and wonder! Members stay engaged even through difficulties and there is an attitude of acceptance for where each member is at in their life. Forum members care without caretaking in a co-dependent way, letting go of their need to be right in favor of simply being present.

To achieve this level of authenticity, members commit to an environment of truth and openness, even when difficult. Forum invites members to stretch and share those parts of life that live *just* beyond their comfort zone.

The Comfort Zone	The Zone of Discomfort	PANIC!
Lowest level of learning while maintaining the status quo takes precedence over all else.	Highest learning possibility. Requires authenticity and willingness to be vulnerable.	Retreat to "fight or flight" behaviors. Self-preservation. Limited learning possible.

There is an understanding that over time trust builds as members make commitments and hold themselves accountable to one another. A willingness to face the fear and discomfort of showing vulnerability ultimately produces a level of caring not found in many relationships. It is often said that members could "take each other down" with the information they hold, but never would.

The Benefits

Belonging to a forum of highly motivated peers calls each member to an even higher level of relational and professional performance. Forum members report a sense of community and connection, as well as growth in their professional leadership and communication skills. In addition, forum provides members a valued venue for gaining clarity and solving personal life issues. As members engage at a high level of authenticity within their forum, the skills and benefits transfer into other areas of their lives, producing a more fun and fulfilling environment at work and at home.

 What do you value most about your forum experience? (Or, what might you most look forward to?)

IT IS ALL ABOUT YOU! *ALL* OF YOU

As you commit to building a forum of friends, you might first want to discover what it means to be a friend to yourself. "Am I a truthful, authentic, and trusting friend with myself?" is a question too few ask or answer. Because, as you look closely, you might discover all the ways you sabotage, betray, and hurt yourself through your thoughts and actions!

In forum, you will bring your "whole person" into a social circle of friends.

	Focus on Internal/Self		
Focus on the Invisible: Being	**Mental Dimension** Values. Principles. Talents. Beliefs. Knowledge. Clarifies, challenges, protects.	**Physical Dimension** Use of time. Discipline. Boundaries. Mission. Care. Self-control. Measurable actions.	**Focus on the Visible: Doing**
	Spiritual Dimension Connection to your creator and creativity. Wonder and appreciation. Your Treasure. Recreation, reflection, and renewal. Aligns with purpose.	**Social Dimension** Relationships. Touch. Passion. Connection to others in community and in serving the greater good. Moves toward a vision.	
	Focus on External/Others		

As you engage with each of these dimensions, you also begin to connect to your sense of well-being across all areas of your life. So, instead of thinking about your "work" life or "home" life, you can think about all of you no matter where you are!

The **Spiritual Dimension** is about your relationship to all that is outside of your "self" but that you cannot see. It's about your understanding and sense of belonging in the mystery, the divine, of God or however you define your Creator and your inherent **purpose** for being. It is your "Why?" The spiritual dimension is about your understanding of why you, everyone, and everything is here and expressing gratitude for all of it. And, just as you are "created" you are also "re-created" through fun and playful pursuits that celebrate the joy of simply being alive. The spiritual dimension is about:

- Living in appreciation for the beauty of all creation.
- **Reflection**, meditation, and prayer.
- Wonder: contemplating the mystery and bigness of the universe.
- Uniqueness: the **treasure** inherent in your individual uniqueness.
- How you experience **joy** and **recreation.**

So, how does this apply in your life?

- **Reflecting Mindfully**: meditation, breathing, prayer and appreciation.
- **Catching joy**: pausing to appreciate simply being you in your playfulness, healthy competition, or the pleasure of an intimate sexual experience.
- **Embracing creativity**: sensing your essence through art, music, dance, sport or creative cooking.
- **Cultivating a sense of belonging:** marking the milestones of life including birthdays, graduations, weddings, and memorials.
- **Breathing** deep and valuing each breath.

A Few Questions to Connect to the Spiritual Dimension

How do you describe your connection to the spiritual? To your most inner being?
What is it you were created for? What is your purpose?
When you are all alone and it's just you, what do you enjoy about you?
What makes you unique? When do you experience your unique creative expression?
When are you most artistic? Creative? Fun? Adventurous? Playful?
What are you celebrating? How are you cultivating a sense of belonging for yourself?
How do you experience joy, gratitude, reflection, and appreciation?

 How do we as a forum support the spiritual well-being of our members?

The **Mental Dimension** is about the internal wiring that guides your day to day activities and behaviors. It's about fundamental beliefs, values, skills, and **principle,** or the rails that set a boundary between "good" and "not good". The mental dimension is also where you make sense of the world around you. As life happens, it is in your mind that you "make up a story" as you assess, evaluate, and apply meaning. It's also where fear lives within you. It's about how you feel at home in your own skin and your commitment to life ideals and values. The mental dimension is about:

- Curiosity, learning, and **knowledge** that protects and equips you.
- Beliefs, values, or principles integrated and updated over a lifetime.
- Moral guiderails, virtues, what it means to live in civil society.
- **Talents** embraced and cultivated.

The mental dimension has a special role in guiding your actions:

- **Making conscious commitments**: Curiosity with all long-held beliefs, committing to 100% responsibility for the results in your life.
- **Willing** to engage with ideas and concepts that are important or challenging.
- **Clarifying** "How We Roll" in all relationships.
- **Seeking** growth, learning, knowledge and new skills.
- **Understanding** the difference between "what has happened" and "what I make what has happened mean."

A Few Questions to Connect to the Mental Dimension

How is your mental clarity? When are you most clear?
What fills your thought life? What do you notice yourself thinking about?
What beliefs are serving you well? Not serving you? What beliefs may want to be challenged?
What are the key life principles that guide your steps every day?
What are you hiding about you? What do you not let the world know?
How are you experiencing anxiety, making future possibilities real, worrying?

 How do we as a forum support the mental well-being of our members?

While it starts with your physical body, the **Physical Dimension** has to do with all of you that is visible and seen. Your **actions**, everything you *do*, including attention to physical well-being, the vocational work that you do, your habits and daily rituals, and how you care for your basic needs of safety and security are included here. This dimension also includes your environment and the physical world in which you live. It's about how you spend your time and how you live out your **mission**. The physical dimension is about:

- Allocation of attention, **time**, and resources.
- The environment you create for home, work, and play.
- Your vocational pursuits, work ethic, and life balance.
- Expression of your emotional experience.

The physical dimension puts all that is "invisible" within you into practice. It is the living out of your purpose and principles through your activities and actions:

- Maintaining **disciplines** around personal habits of **self-care** and well-being.
- Exercising self-control and balancing rest with activity.
- Choosing work that aligns with your best self.
- Attending to areas where you are in-balanced or tolerating less than optimal conditions. Paying attention to **measurable** results.
- Establishing clear agreements and sticking to them.

A Few Questions to Connect to the Physical Dimension

What is your sense of self-care? What words describe your relationship with your body?
How is your home and work environment? What are you tolerating or enjoying?
Describe your balance of work, rest, eating, and other activities. Are you satisfied?
How satisfying are the challenges and rewards of daily life?
Where are your actions aligned or out of alignment with your purpose and beliefs?
Where do you have crossed-boundaries, injustices, resentments? Where are you giving yourself away?

 How do we as a forum support the physical well-being of our members?

The **Social Dimension** is about your relationships and how you bring your whole self to engage in community with others. It is living and sharing responsibilities in small groups, practicing good stewardship for all that has been entrusted to you, and providing service with others toward the greater good. The social dimension is about:

- Connection: the intimate relationships with loved ones, your circle of friends, and the world beyond.
- **Touch:** the way you interact and touch the lives of others.
- Your **vision:** What you are aiming for in life and the legacy you leave.
- How you build "social capital" and the strength of society.
- Your **passion**. The future that you long for and create.

As with the physical dimension, the social dimension is about your actions, but with the added components of "with whom?" and "toward what end?" You are hard-wired to connect with others. The social dimension is put into practice through:

- **Connecting** in **authentic** relationships. Speaking your courageous truth and allowing yourself to be fully seen with others.
- **Serving** some greater purpose to improve the human condition.
- **Engaging** with people different than you and expanding your world view.

Effective leaders embrace the notion of holistic well-being, recognizing that the pursuit of balance and maturity includes all dimensions of life. Forum members embrace a whole life view of themselves and challenge one another to grow in meaningful, purposeful, and transformational ways.

A few questions to connect to the Social Dimension

How is your connection to the people most important to you?
Which relationships are working well? Which relationships need some attention?
Where are you experiencing a sense of community or common cause?
What is it you are moving toward in your life? What is your vision?
How are you connected to or serving something bigger than yourself?
Where are you experiencing loss, grief, or letting go?
How are you expressing and accepting love in your life?

 How do we as a forum support the social well-being of our members?

CLEAR AND CLEAN COMMUNICATION

Successful forums communicate well. Crisp check-ins, updates, and explorations require a basic understanding of clear and clean communication skills. Some definitions:

Data	Recordable **facts**. Objective observations. Measurable results.
Judgments	What we make data mean. Our analysis, opinions, or beliefs about the facts. Fiction, or "The story I make up". "My truth" but not THE truth.
Feelings	Self-generated anger, fear, sadness, joy, or other emotions.
Wants	Desires, requests, proposals.
Clear	The communicator is clear on their want, desire, request or proposal!
Clean	The communicator takes 100% responsibility for their part in the relationship. Judgments are owned. Emotions are acknowledged and expressed without blame. Data is presented without analysis.

Why is this important?

Effective leaders separate fact from fiction and see the difference between "what has happened" and "what I make what has happened mean." Data is just data. We can argue about the facts and recognize that there might be differing versions of the facts, but your judgments, feelings, and wants are yours. They are inarguable truths. No can say "You don't think that!" or "You don't feel that way!" even if they don't agree with your feeling or thought. And so, you get to take 100% responsibility in owning your judgments, feelings, and wants! They are yours. When exploring an issue this distinction allows all involved to remain curious and to speak openly without attack or defensiveness. We each commit to staying clean, taking 100% responsibility for our part in every relationship.

Let's go a little further into each of these.

Data/Facts: An exact description of the behavior or events in question. Think of data as what an aerial drone could record without any interpretation or analysis. Data describes action, activity, or a result.

- "It is 11:00am."
- "Three forum members have explored issues at meetings this year."
- "You agreed to make a call and did not do so."

Common Mis-Speak	Example	Coaching Tip	Clean Communication
Unclear or unspecific information.	"I'm out of money."	Clarify. State the specific facts.	"I have $2,000 in my checking account and $5,000 in bills to pay."
Mixing a judgment, opinion, or feeling with data.	"You're late again!"	"Late" is a judgment based on a previous agreement. Better to communicate the specific data first.	"We agreed to start at 11:00 and you got here at 11:15."
Confusing data with judgment.	"The facts are that we didn't do a good job on that."	Is there some data to draw upon that would define "good"?	"We agreed to a 3-minute update and half of us exceeded the agreed upon time."

 What are some examples of data mis-speak that you have seen or heard in your group? In your work?

Judgments: A thought, assessment, opinion, observation, or belief. A judgment is "your truth". It's not "THE TRUTH". Judgments are "what we make data mean" or the story we make up from the data before us. The invitation is to always own our judgments as simply our judgments. You know you are owning your judgments when you speak from the "I" or "My."

- "My judgment is that…"
- "My opinion, thought, belief is…"
- "When that happened, the story I made up was…"

Common Mis-Speak	Example	Coaching Tip	Clean Communication
Confusing thoughts/judgments and feelings.	"I feel like we've really messed this up."	Using the word "like" or "that" after the word "feel" usually indicates a judgment.	"My belief is that we've messed this up.
Expressing a judgment without owning it.	"You're angry."	Own that as an assessment of the situation.	"I think you're angry," or, "I notice you seem angry here."
	"You are wrong about that!"	Own your opinion.	"I'm not in agreement with you on that. I have a different opinion."
The unsupported or un-owned assertion.	"Everyone would think that…"	What is it that you think?	"I think that…"
	"It's a hard thing to do."	How is it for you?	"It is very hard for me."

 When someone says something is true about you, is it true? So, what is it?

Feelings: An emotion around whatever it is that you are communicating. The four primary emotions are joy, sadness, anger, and fear. Feelings are also "your truth" in that they are inarguable. Emotions simply are what they are.

- "I feel sad right now."
- "I felt angry."
- "It brings me joy."
- "I've got some fear coming up."

Common Mis-Speak	Example	Coaching Tip	Clean Communication
Expressing an assessment or judgment as an emotion.	"I feel betrayed."	Words that end in "ed" are usually not feelings but judgments. Own your judgment of how you are and express the feeling.	"When I judge that I have been betrayed, I feel very sad."
Holding someone else responsible for our emotions.	"This makes me mad!" "You make me mad!"	Own the feeling as something you are self-generating.	"I feel mad." "I feel mad when you…"
Making emotional soup.	"When I hear you singing like that, I feel a little jealous. I mean, I feel happy too, because you are happy, but I feel a little bit angry that I don't have that talent."	Narrow it down to the one primary emotion.	"When you sang like that, I felt sad."

 What emotions are you most comfortable expressing? Least comfortable?

Wants: A statement of desire, a truth about what is going on inside of you or a request for someone else. Stating a desire sets a clean boundary and prevents guessing by the other person. And, it's simply your "want" - no promises on the outcome.

- "My desire is…"
- "My request/proposal is…"
- "What I want here is…"

Common Mis-Speak	Example	Coaching Tip	Clean Communication
Unclear, unspecific statements.	"I want to be respected."	Be specific. State what could be said or done to show respect.	"So, what I want is, when we agree to meet at 11:00, I want you to be here, ready to meet, at 11:00."
Confusing "needs" with "wants."	"I really *need* to do that."	Needs include food, clothing, air, water. Own the want as simply a want.	"I want to do that." "I commit to do that." "I will do that."
	"I *need* to say…"		"What I want to say is…"
Stating what you "don't want"	"I don't want to be stuck here."	State what you DO want.	"I want to move forward with my life."
Projecting a desire on to someone else.	"I just want what is best for you."	Clarify what you really want for you or what you get from your want.	"I want you to eat well so that you stay healthy and I don't miss work to take care of you."
Using a question when something is desired of someone else.	"Do you think I am attractive?" "Don't you think everyone would too?"	Make a request.	"I'd really like some affirmation right now. I am feeling vulnerable."

 How is a request or proposal different than a demand?

PROHIBITED WORDS

Some words in our language have been over-used such that their meaning has been lost. Other words are non-committal and don't really mean anything at all. Effective forums desire meaningful dialogue and communication. There is a desire to use words that mean something!

LESS MEANING	MORE MEANING
I'm good!	I feel joyful. I feel grateful and proud. I am not open to sharing right now. I have an issue to clear.
I'm sorry.	I own my mistake. I feel sad when you are hurting. I feel bad for what I've done.
Please forgive me.	How can I repair our agreement? How can I make this right?
Everything is fine.	I feel overwhelmed. My fear is off the chart right now.
I'm not mad.	There is a part of me that is angry. I feel ___.
I'll try to do that.	I commit to doing that. I choose to do that. I choose not to do that.
I want to be more committed.	My commitment is to… Our agreement then is to…

 What words do you use when you are trying to say nothing?

UNPACKING ANY ISSUE

Anytime you want to unpack or make sense of a situation or issue in forum (or in life!) you do well to start with the facts and then generate the associated thoughts and emotions. In this journey you might get clarity on **what you want** before determining a course of action!

To unpack, first make sure you are "in": Some issues might be risky, vulnerable, or exposing. Check to be sure that you are ready to engage:

- What might be the risk of exploring this topic or issue?
- What might be the benefit?
- What long-held beliefs might come into play? What beliefs might want to be put on hold for a time of exploration?
- Are you willing to take the risk and move forward?

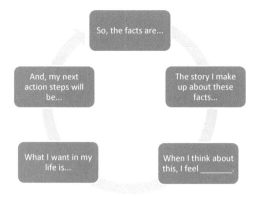

Start with the facts: Always start with a presentation of data ("just the facts"). **Facts are observable and quantifiable**. Facts are not feelings. Facts are not thoughts.

- What has happened? Who? What? When? Where? How Many?
- Is there general agreement on the data by all parties? Are there differing versions of the facts?

The next step is to consider questions that help make sense of the data and discover your **thoughts** and beliefs.

- What do you think? What do you make the data mean?
- What is most significant?

- What "stories" might you make up from this data? How does this data affect your view of the future?
- What is *your darkest story about you* attached to this issue?
- What do you know about yourself (your dysfunctions, sabotaging patterns) that might be in play in this issue?
- How does this challenge your values, long-held beliefs, or principles?
- Are there different perspectives? Is there an *opposite story* that might also be true?
- How might "the other side" view the data?
- What has blocked you from exploring this in the past?
- What can you learn from this? What are the implications?

And then, uncover the **emotional undercurrent**.

- When you think about this issue, what emotions come up? Where do you feel it in your body?
- How is fear of the future or the unknown at play? What if you had no fear?
- How is anger or frustration present? Have any boundaries been crossed?
- What has been lost? What might need to be grieved?
- What has been gained? What might be celebrated? For what are you thankful?

Once the data, thoughts, and feelings have been flushed out, take a moment to get quiet with yourself to let your thoughts go and feelings be. Feel fully. And then, the discussion shifts to **"what do you want?"**

- What do you really want? What is it that you do not have now?
- And if you had that, what would you really have?
- What is the risk of getting what you want? What might it mean?
- How do your wants align with your bigger purposes? Is there a deeper want?
- What might others have to say about this want?
- What else might you want?
- What might you let go of in order to get this want?
- Where might action or inaction lead to in the future?

Once your **"clear wants"** are discovered, move into the tactical step of **"clean action."**

- How might your wants inform your actions? What will you do?
- What are your options?
- What support would be helpful and useful?
- Who will you be accountable to?
- What will success look like?

SUMMARY – UNPACKING ANY ISSUE

Honor your care and concern for yourself!	I'm noticing that I am emotionally reacting, and I'd like to get clear with myself about…
What is the recordable data? No judgments or analysis.	The specific **facts** are…
What are your most critical judgments, opinions, analysis, beliefs… the dark story you make up about you?	The **fictional** story I make up about these facts is…
What are your emotions? Angry, Sad, Joyful, Afraid, Also: Ashamed, Guilty, Numb	When I think about this, I **feel**…
What are your known dysfunctional behaviors, sabotaging patterns, chronic compulsions, protective strategies… That all help create and sustain the issue?	My part in this is…
What are your desired outcomes, or what you want to release or let go for yourself (and not just the others involved).	And, I specifically want…

Read it out loud. Check for accuracy. Is there more?

Plan your next step. What will you do? Consider any or all:

Offer and Counter-Offer	*Develop options on resolving the real issue with yourself. What might you do irrespective of what anyone else does?*
Apologies and Amends	*Offer meaningful apology to yourself! Feel fully. Generate some self-compassion for being where you are. Ask yourself, "How can I make it right with me?"*
Systems, Structure, and Norms Reflection	*What systems (ways of doing things), structures (environments, tools, relationships), or norms (agreements for outcomes, agenda, roles, responsibilities) might you put in place or change for yourself? With others?*

SECTION II: FORUM NORMS AND GUIDELINES

Successful forums operate with a structured set of guidelines and expectations. Commonly, norms are created in the following areas:

1. Shared Mission/Vision

2. Confidentiality

3. Commitment/Attendance/Punctuality

4. Protocol/Respect Guidelines

5. Membership
    a. Size
    b. New Members
    c. Members Resigning
    d. Conflicts of Interest

6. Leadership/Moderator's Term

7. Meetings/Structure
    a. Venue/Food/Alcohol
    b. Timing/Frequency
    c. Agenda (Updates, Presentations, Discussions)
    d. Host/Payment
    e. Emergency Meetings

8. Launching and Renewal
    a. Retreats and Resource Facilitation
    b. New Forum Checklist
    c. Important Forum Moments
    d. Evaluating Forum Strength

The following pages provide questions and thoughts to consider when establishing guidelines and norms for your forum. A two-page document template is also available at www.theprincipalsforum.org.

MISSION AND VISION FOR FORUM

Every forum creates its own mission and vision… its own statement of what will be done (Mission) and how each member will be different because of their involvement (Vision).

Examples

"Our Mission is to create a caring group of committed peers and friends, meeting on a regular basis for safe, unforced sharing on business and personal topics. Our forum exists in an environment of mutual trust, integrity and tenderness, where members are truthful with one another, offering and receiving counsel, holding one another accountable, and pointing out blind spots. Our vision is to grow together through a blend of presentations, discussions, exercises, experiences, adventures, celebrations… and pure fun."

~~~

"Our forum focuses on three areas… Education, Experiences, and Entertainment. Our time is split 40% on Business/Skills development, 40% on Personal Transparency and Awareness, and 20% Social. Our vision is that we will deepen our commitment to one another and to our own personal best."

~~~

"Our mission is to gather a caring group of committed peers and friends and create a place for the best and most challenging parts of our lives to be shared. Our forum is a place of safety and confidentiality where we can explore the sometimes difficult issues of work and personal life. Our vision is to grow together through discussions, experiences, adventures, celebrations and pure fun. Our hope is to grow as people and as a circle of friends.

~~~

"Our forum is a place of safety and confidentiality where we explore the sometimes difficult issues of work and personal life. Our hope is to grow as people and as a circle of friends."

Good Mission and Vision Discussion Questions

How do we define ourselves as a forum? What makes us distinct from other groups in our lives?

How do we each desire to grow or change from our forum involvement?

Most forum activities fall into one of three categories:

Personal Growth/Awareness 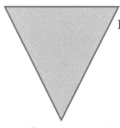 Business/Life Problem Solving

Social/Recreational Activity

What is our desired priority or mix?

Our Forum Mission is to_____

_____

Our Vision is to _____

_____

_____

CONFIDENTIALITY

"Confidentiality is the number one concern and the absolute requirement for my forum experience." (A Forum Member)

Enough cannot be said about the importance of confidentiality in forum. Nothing can kill the sense of safety and support in a forum like a breach of confidentiality. It is important to note however that there is no legal protection inherent in the forum relationship, including those of "mandated reporters" or "client privilege".

- *Recommended Norm: Forum members are assured that any information shared will be held in complete confidence by the other members. What is discussed in the meeting room … stays in the room.*

Thankfully, breaches of confidentiality are rare. In case of a breach, the following steps are recommended:

1. The person making the breach, or involved in a "near miss", immediately brings the issue forward to the individual involved and the moderator.

2. Any alleged violation of confidentiality reported to the moderator is investigated and reported at the next scheduled meeting.

3. The member making the breach is expected to offer their resignation to the forum.

4. If the moderator is suspected of a confidentiality breach, the group will choose an interim moderator until the issue is resolved.

5. The decision to accept the resignation of the individual involved is made by group vote, based on the damage done.

Confidentiality Case Studies

1. Sylvia returns home after a meeting and her partner asks "How was it?" Which statements maintain confidentiality?

- _____ "Well, I learned that I'm not as screwed up as I thought after listening to the group."
- _____ "It was positive and productive for me. I'm learning about my need to control…"

- _____ "It was positive, except for one member who really bugs me the way they derail things."

2. You run into a forum member at a business association meeting. Which statements maintain confidentiality?

- _____ "After last week's meeting we really should be praying for (forum member) Nick."
- _____ "Your presentation last week really hit a chord with me. I'd like to talk more with you…"
- _____" What do you think of (forum member) Mary's new deal?"

3. During a presentation, Kaley reports that she is about to fire a key employee, who has no idea about what is coming. You know the individual about to be fired through your local soccer club and have a valued social relationship with their family. What do you do?

4. A forum member is engaging in what you judge to be harmful drug use. It has come up several times in forum, and you are noticing your own anger about it. What do you do?

5. Fred shared in forum that he was worried about his wife's pregnancy… She seemed to be sick all the time and longer than normal. At a party with the chapter, (forum mate) Marco asked Fred's wife if she was feeling better. Fred and his wife then left in a hurry - they'd had bad news about the baby. How might Marco have handled this interaction in a way that preserved confidentiality?

6. Vidmar belongs to two forums that both maintain comparable norms around confidentiality. He is having an issue with a member in one of the forums and would like to do a presentation in the other Forum about it to seek guidance. He is unsure how to maintain confidentiality. How can he maintain confidentiality?

(?) **Given what you know about the social, financial, civic, and vocational intertwining of our forum, what are some potential areas of concern around confidentiality? How might a "near miss" occur?**

What are our specific agreements around confidentiality?

COMMITMENT/ATTENDANCE/PUNCTUALITY

Membership in forum is a privilege and it is expected that all members give forum meetings priority.

Because forums are peer-based and often self-moderated, it is common for members to not enforce attendance and punctuality norms out of a desire to avoid conflict. In experience though, adherence to forum attendance and punctuality norms reduces tension and conflict by having a pre-set agreement. Power plays by members with a need to stand-out or be treated as "special" are minimized. (See Forum Support Section and "Keeping the Air Clear" Model).

Recommended Norms:

- *The forum calendar is set between 3-months to a year in advance.*

- *Meetings begin with a "soft start" of 15-30 minutes to allow for arrivals, settling in, and social time. At the appointed "hard start" time, the meeting starts. Members understand and agree that punctuality and staying to the end of the meeting is a priority.*

- *Members unable to attend accept responsibility to inform the moderator, or his / her designate, by noon the day before the meeting.*

- *Each member commits to missing no more than two meetings per year, unless otherwise excused by the group (e.g., extended travel, illness). If a member misses more than two meetings, the other members may meet to discuss his / her commitment and continued membership.*

- *Members missing a meeting agree to contact each other member prior to the next meeting, exchanging updates with the other members to stay current with forum and member issues.*

Some forums initiate a financial penalty for late arrival. Other forums agree that any member more than 15 minutes late should not attend, out of respect for those able to show up on time. Successful forums understand the importance of punctuality and practice an "on-time" discipline.

What is our current behavior telling us about our commitment to attendance and punctuality? Is it working for us?

What about life changes? How do we want to handle a work move, new relationship that affects attendance, uncontrollable events in a forum members life?

What are our specific agreements around attendance and punctuality?

PROTOCOL/RESPECT GUIDELINES

Successful forums operate in an environment of respect… respect for self and for one another. Behavior guidelines create a level playing field for all.

Recommended / Sample Guidelines:

1. I will respect confidentiality… what is said in the room stays in the room.
   What is our agreement about confidentiality? Precisely, what can we share and with whom?

2. I will be present in the moment… keeping electronics off and clearing thoughts and issues.
   What distracts you the most? What helps you stay present in the moment?

3. I will stay around when times get tough…the ability to keep the air clear and resolve conflict strengthens forum.
   What topic might you avoid if you were concerned the forum might not be around when times got tough?

4. I will be on time and stay until the end…because I respect you.
   How does punctuality show up in my life? How do we want to create a norm of punctuality in forum?

5. I will ask for what I want… and recognize that I don't always get what I want.
   What keeps me from asking for what I want? Who do I need to ask, "What do you want?"

6. I will own and speak my truth…because my level of revealing increases depth in our group.
   What truth have I been holding? How could I share it?

7. I am willing to laugh and be patient with myself and each other… as we find our way.
   How do I screw up? What would it look like to laugh at myself and be patient in that situation?

8. *I will own my feelings and judgments...because they are mine.*
   What are the risks I perceive to sharing my feelings? My judgments?

9. I will listen to feedback with openness and curiosity... regardless of how it is delivered.
   When do I act defensively? What are my telling signs that I am defensive?

10. I will not blame, shame or fix others...and take 100% responsibility for my part in every relationship.
    When I feel blamed, shamed or fixed, how do I react?

11. I will ask permission before offering thoughts, advice or observations...and do so with compassion.
    What would change in our forum if we asked permission before offering each other feedback?

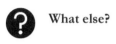 **What else?**

Make this list yours! Edit it. Pare it down. What is most important to you?

Resource: Kaley Warner Klemp explores small group guidelines in great detail in her booklet *"Thirteen Guidelines for Effective Teams"* available on www.kaleyklemp.com.

MEMBERSHIP AND CONFLICT OF INTEREST

Unlike an informal group of friends, and to achieve the levels of confidentiality and safety desired, forums operate on a closed- or fixed- roster basis.

Most forums maintain membership at 6-9 members. Forums with fewer than 6 members struggle with shared responsibilities and are vulnerable to collapse in cases of absence. Forums with greater than 9 members struggle to provide enough air time for all members.

Many forums add new members two at a time and do so with some form of welcoming process (see Forum Tools section).

Most forums expect resigning members to give adequate notice to attend a final meeting to bring closure to the experience for all.

Successful forums carefully manage the power dynamic between members and establish expectations aimed at avoiding conflicts of interest, including:

- *Forum members are discouraged from significant business relationships, investing in each other's businesses, or maintaining any mutual interest. It is agreed that any potential conflict of interest is disclosed and cleared with the forum.*

- *No competitive business interests will exist within the forum.*

- *No spouses or partners in forum.*

- *Any member creating a conflict of interest is expected to disclose it and offer their resignation to the forum.*

Most forums recognize that there may be cases where conflict of interest may be difficult to determine. Examples to consider:

1. A forum member owns a company that provides security and alarm systems for corporate offices and provides services to several forum members. Is this a conflict?

2. Through the course of the forum experience, a member hears many positive things about a key employee of a fellow member and decides to quietly recruit the employee to come to their company. Does this create a conflict of interest?

3. A high profile and high net worth forum member has decided to invest in a start-up company and invites other forum members to also invest.

The underlying principle… forums function best when all members are disinterested in the affairs of all other members.

 What makes sense for our forum?

FORUM LEADERSHIP

Forum leadership is a shared experience. All members assume rotating responsibilities, with two or three members elected for leadership roles at any time.

Moderator
- Manages the forum calendar.
- Facilitates meeting format, conversations and explorations. Upholds Forum norms.
- Engages with members to identify issues to explore, generative discussions, and observations. Invites member participation.
- Manages resolution of any conflicts of interest or breaches of confidentiality.
- Models clear and clean communication.
- Guides the forum to higher levels of authenticity, commitment, openness, and trust.
- Attends forum community events and leadership trainings as able.
- Delegates tasks to ensure shared leadership for the forum.
- Conducts annual evaluation.
- Consults with chapter officers and resource facilitator.

Effective moderators are committed, open, and able to speak directly. They are self-assured, thoughtful, and enthusiastic. Effective moderators build a sense of community and are flexible in adapting to forum needs.

Assistant Moderator/Coach
- Moderates monthly meetings in the absence of the moderator.
- Serves as exploration coach as requested. Works with moderator to manage the parking lot and invites members to participate in explorations and discussions.
- Models clear and clean communication.
- Attends Moderator Training Workshop.
- Supports the moderator as requested.

The Term for both the moderator and assistant moderator is typically 12 months. Election is by secret ballot with no nomination or campaign process. The outgoing moderator simply asks each member to write on a piece of paper the name of the member each believes is best prepared to serve in this role. The member receiving the most votes is declared the new moderator, and second most the assistant moderator. Members desiring to serve as moderator are encouraged to vote for themselves!

Forum Administrator

Many forums designate a member as administrator to perform a variety of duties in support of the forum, including:

- Manages forum funds.
- Keeps forum norms and guidelines updated and followed.
- Produces meeting notices and announcements.
- Keeps forum roster updated.
- Coordinates with rotating day host to ensure adequate preparations.

Rotating Responsibilities
The following duties may be designated and rotated for each meeting:

Day Host: Secures venue, arranges food and refreshments, conducts meeting welcome and opening.

Exploration Coach: A member selected by the moderator or a presenter who conducts either a pre-meeting coaching session or an impromptu coaching session at the meeting for an exploration, and moderates at the meeting. (See worksheets in Forum Tools section).

Process Observer/Timekeeper: Manages time during updates and presentations. Provides feedback on clear communication and use of protocol.

Retreat Chair: Chooses a retreat committee, and secures venue and resource facilitator, designs agenda, and manages logistics.

MEETING STRUCTURE

Venue/Food/Alcohol: The preferred venue for forum meetings is a private room with comfortable seating and **no table**, so that members may sit in a circle without barriers. Many forums choose a consistent venue for all meetings. A private home living room is ideal but only if other family members are elsewhere! Food should be adequate for the time of day and need not be extravagant. Alcohol is typically only served as a meal beverage and only after the conclusion of the formal meeting.

Timing/Frequency: Eight or nine monthly meetings through the year are typical. Time of day is dependent on group needs, travel distances, and other commitments. Many forums conclude their three-hour meeting with a meal.

Agenda (Updates, Explorations, Discussions): Most forums agree to follow the "Recommended Meeting Outline" as presented in the next section.

Host/Payment: The day host typically takes care of all payments and may be reimbursed through the forum treasury. An option is to set a budget for meeting costs and be sure that all members host one meeting during the year so that each member is bearing roughly the same expense.

Emergency Meetings: Any member may call an emergency meeting to present on a critical or urgent issue. Attendance at emergency meetings is requested but not required.

Norms:
- *The forum will meet ____ times during the year. All regular meetings follow the recommended meeting format.*
- *Meetings are held in private areas, free from distraction. Alcohol is only served as a meal beverage.*
- *An emergency meeting may be called by any member to address a specific issue. Attendance at emergency meetings is not mandatory.*

FORUM RENEWAL

Successful forums understand the value of getting away for a time of recreation and renewal. Playing together is an important part of how we celebrate the friendships and community we value. Activities specifically designed for recreation and renewal create a time and space for:

- Celebration of accomplishments... and expressions of gratitude.
- Fun... friendly competition, outdoor adventures, creative expressions.
- Reconnection to self and soul... reflection and rest.

Forum retreats are also a time to focus on personal awareness and growth as well as increasing the levels of safety and authenticity in the forum. Most forums engage a resource facilitator to design their retreat experience from beginning to end with this express purpose in mind. Recommended norms:

- *A strength evaluation is conducted annually.*

- *Our forum maintains an ongoing relationship with a resource facilitator to stay abreast of emerging best practices and provide "tune-up" support.*

- *Our forum organizes an annual retreat and utilizes an outside resource facilitator at least every other year.*

 What is our commitment regarding forum evaluation?

What might we accomplish on a retreat together that might add value to our regular meetings? What might be the blocks to an annual retreat?

NEW FORUM CHECKLIST

New forums benefit from a thoughtful progression of experiences that ultimately produce high levels of vulnerability and trust.

- Create you Forum Vision (Page 21) and Guidelines (Page 27). Develop other norms.

- Create a ritual to share your stories
    - Bring pictures of important people or times in your life and share
    - Do a "Walk in Time" exercise
    - Do a Conversation Round

- Gain understanding of Clear Communication skills (Page 9)

- Become proficient at Forum Explorations
    - Have each person coach and present

- Practice protocol
    - Practice forum support tools (clearing issues at various levels)

- Confirm forum roles
    - Identify Forum Administrator
    - Determine Moderator tenure

- Choose a forum name

- Celebrate your launch!

What's next?

Once you have completed the above, add to your toolkit…

- Practice Generative Discussions (Page 66) or Member Inner-View (Page 72)
- Focus on a group issue, unclear agreement, or missed expectation (Page 85)
- Share experiences and advice in appropriate context (Page 100)
- Become proficient at navigating emotion (Page 103)

SPECIAL MOMENTS IN FORUM

Effective forums recognize the importance of special moments, including:

Launching a New Forum Year

- Review and recommit to forum norms
- Disclose and resolve any conflicts of interest that may exist.
- Conduct an in-depth "Whole Life Inventory" (Page 50) and identify the top three or four significant topics for each member.
- Establish calendar.
- Set an intention for the forum year. "How do we want to be different as a forum a year from now?"
- Do Walk in Time exercise in a new or different way.

Saying Good Bye

- Departing members are always invited to a closing meeting.
- Do an appreciation round inviting each member to share a story, a moment of appreciation, a learning from the departing member.
- Give a token of remembrance to the departing member.

Saying Hello

- Anytime a member joins forum, it is a new forum. Everything starts over.
- In the presence of new members, share "my favorite" moments in the "old" forum, remembering to preserve confidentiality!
- Ritualize the ending of the old forum. Light a candle at the beginning of the meeting and blow it out after story-sharing and an appreciation round.

Members in Crisis

Life happens. When forum members experience a crisis, it is important for the moderator and forum members to discuss appropriate support and response, recognizing that forum is not "family" or "work." We're not therapists. We're friends at the deepest level. Forums may hold emergency meetings (with or without the member) for this purpose.

FORUM STRENGTH

Effective forums evaluate their performance on a regular basis and take steps to improve. Assign a score of 1-4 for each item and total at the bottom.

1. Very weak. Not done.
2. Weak but trying. Not an area of strength
3. Evident and strong. Done on a fairly regular basis. Not an area of concern.
4. Very strong. Done all the time.

Organization:	Score:
1. Forum Mission/Vision Statement is current and relevant.	
2. Forum Norms are written, followed, and been reviewed in the past year.	
3. Leadership is shared. Every member has served as moderator, coach, process observer or day/retreat host within the past year.	
4. Calendar is followed. Meetings are held as planned with no more than two cancelled or rescheduled meetings per year.	
5. Confidentiality is maintained. High levels of trust are evidenced by all members sharing at a vulnerable level.	
6. There are at least six and no more than ten members in the Forum.	
7. Members disclose any real or possible conflicts of interest in a timely manner.	
8. Forum strength evaluation is completed at least once each year with the results reported to forum trainer and members.	
Meetings:	
9. Meeting logistics/reminders are distributed by the host (or moderator) two or three days ahead of each meeting.	
10. Members arrive on time; meetings start and end on time.	
11. Members show respect to moderator and one another, and are attentive while others are speaking. Electronics are off.	
12. Forum business at regular meetings is kept brief and pertinent for all.	
13. Member check-ins and updates are crisp and pertinent. The parking lot is created monthly and monitored for progress.	
14. Meetings hold the interest of members. Explorations and discussions are meaningful with take home value for all.	
15. Protocol guidelines are followed. Experience is shared over advice. Judgments are owned. Members participate equally.	
16. The forum meets monthly. Attendance is at or near 100%.	
17. Meeting venue allows for comfortable seating, privacy, and minimal interruption.	

Forum Spirit:	
18. Members feel a sense of pride and commitment to the forum.	
19. Members refrain from doing business with other forum members.	
20. Members are comfortable discussing personal beliefs, feelings, and issues.	
21. Issues with group members or the group as a whole are cleared in a timely manner.	
22. Social contact with members outside of forum meetings supports forum strength.	
Forum Outcomes:	
23. Members feel a sense of community and connection to one another as a result of participation.	
24. Members experience growth with both professional and personal value.	
25. Forum is a valued venue for gaining clarity and/or solving business and personal life issues.	
TOTAL SCORE	

A total score of ___ might indicate:

85-100   You have excellent forum strength. A model to others.
75-85   You have a forum worth being a part of. You are successful and strong. Keep it up!
65-75   You have some areas to improve. Pick some key items and focus on improvement.
< 65   You may need help. Ask for it. Talk to your resource facilitator.

SECTION III: FORUM MEETINGS

Effective forum meetings are the key ingredient to forum success. Time invested in planning meetings which run on time, are interesting, and have a sense of purpose will result in greater commitment by all members. All forum meetings share these basic components:

TIME	ACTIVITY	RESPONSIBILITY
5 minutes	**Opening**	Day Host (if assigned) provides a reading, electronics check, logistics instructions.
10 minutes	**Check-In and Clearing**	Moderator provides structure or instructions for check-in and clearing any issues.
10 minutes	**Conversation Starter**	Moderator poses a thoughtful whole life question that helps shift the altitude from the "here and now" to the bigger story.
50 minutes	**Member Updates and Parking Lot (Page 50)**	Moderator provides structure using a written handout or question. A timekeeper may be designated. 3-5 minutes per member followed by a brief "I notice" round. Response limited to "thank you." Moderator poses question and builds parking lot with levels of urgency.
15 minutes	**Break**	Members engage socially. Limited electronic use. Moderator (with Assistant Moderator or coach) determines agenda for remainder of meeting.
60 minutes	**Explorations and Discussions**	Moderator, assistant moderator, and/or coach provides leadership.
15 minutes	**Business**	Moderator or other members with forum business to conduct.
15 minutes	**Closing**	All share learnings, action plans, and appreciations. Clear the air as necessary.
Roughly 3 hours	**Adjournment**	Members leave or adjourn for a social meal.

The following pages highlight each section in greater detail.

Opening: A formal opening creates a boundary that says we are now moving from our everyday life into a special place where forum norms will guide behavior. The opening need not vary from one meeting to the next and is often best when known and repetitive.

1. A synchronized "turning off" of all electronics.

2. A time of silence or mindful breathing for all forum members to let go of thoughts and get present.

3. The reading of a poem or thought for the day.

4. A brief review of key forum guidelines.

Check-In: The "check-in" gives each member the opportunity to verbally state that they are present and ready to be with the group.

1. The first check-in is always brief ("3 or 4 words to describe how you are feeling right now") and may be in response to a question ("One word each to describe how you are mentally, physically, spiritually and socially?"). The check-in always ends with the statement "I'm in!" as a declaration that "my attention is fully here and I release all distractions."

2. A second follow up question may also be used: "What might keep you from being fully present?" This is an opportunity for any member to report any "fires currently burning" in their life that they wish to release for the duration of the meeting.

3. The third check-in question is designed to clear any issues draining energy or present in the group: "Are there any issues with yourself, with another member, or with the group as a whole that need to be cleared?" Members individually respond with the statement "I am clear" or "I would like to clear the air with…" (See Keeping the Air Clear Summary on Page 85).

Conversation Starter: A responsive question after the check in gives all members the opportunity to "shift their altitude" to the bigger picture of their life. Responses are brief and do not include questions or discussion. (See Page 126 for sample questions.)

Member Updates and Parking Lot: Each member is given an opportunity to share in a structured but uninterrupted way. Effective forums embrace the notion that the update **is not** for the group's benefit. The update is for each member to give some airtime to the most meaningful and significant parts of their life. Updates help us look more closely at the issues which might be holding us back, or the opportunities that are being presented to us. A common complaint of ineffective forums is that meetings simply become "extended updates" where one or more members monopolize time by sharing in exhausting detail. Effective forums establish a time limit for updates, and use a written structure for sharing (see Pages 52-54 for samples).

After each member update, the floor is opened for a few members to "notice" what has been heard following a specific structure:

"I noticed you…"
"I notice the connection of what you shared today with a prior update…"
"When you spoke about _____, I felt _____."

The member being noticed is not expected to respond with anything other than "thank you." The purpose of the "I Notice Round" is to encourage active and engaged listening **and** for all members to feel accepted and heard.

The moderator then asks the member for one issue to place in the Forum Parking Lot. The parking lot includes the most pertinent and pressing issues in each member's life. Building the parking lot at each meeting provides a focused opportunity for all members to reflect on what has been said and heard while identifying the top current issues in their lives. The moderator may select one of the following questions:

"What is the top issue in your life right now?"
"If you were to explore an issue today, what would it be?"
"What did you come here today to get insight or clarity on?"

In building the parking lot, each member may also be asked to rate the level of urgency of the issue (1 low to 4 being highest and most urgent).

After all members have given their updates and the parking lot built, each member is invited to complete the statement "If I were the moderator, I would invite _____ to explore _____ issue."

Break: The break provides an opportunity for members to connect socially around common issues or desires. The moderator may specify a limited time for checking electronics/phones. While the group breaks, the moderator reflects on what has been shared thus far, and determines the agenda for the balance of the meeting.

Member Explorations and Discussions: Based on what has been shared or any pre-planned items, the moderator uses their discretion in crafting the second half of the meeting to be meaningful and significant for all members. Effective Forum Moderators pick the best tool for the job!

Forum Tool	When to Use
Exploring in the River: Connecting to the Emotional undercurrent (page 56)	A member is seeking to understand an issue or dynamic in their lives. There are often significant stories with emotional attachments, including fears, angers or dissatisfactions, the sadness of loss, or excitement about a possible future. Members are willing to engage at exploring the undercurrent without a specific destination in mind.
In-Forum Exploration: Discovering the Deeper Want (page 59)	A member is seeking clarity in a specific issue or decision in their life. There are often multiple options and perspectives. Members have shared experiences that might bring insight to the presenting member. A coach is used to guide the member through a thoughtful inquiry.
The Brainstorming Session: "I know what I want. What should I do?" (page 65)	A member is clear on their desired outcome or future condition. They have explored the blocks, risks, and any factors keeping them stuck or in their present condition. Forum members are able to provide ideas, insights, and suggestions without becoming attached to their solution for the member.
Forum Generative Discussion: Stimulating action for all members. (page 66)	A topic is relevant to many forum members and there may be differences of opinion. There is a desire for shared commitment to action and accountability in forum.
"How is that Working for You?" Exposing Unconscious Commitments. (page 70)	A member is stuck in a cycle of coping, blaming or complaining about a specific issue or dynamic in their life. The member has said "It's not working for me!" but things don't change. Forum members are open to providing difficult feedback to the member in a respectful way.
The Member Inner-View: Befriending the parts of us we don't like. (page 72)	A member is falling into an old pattern or behavior, one that they have identified as a problem in their life. Member desires to engage with this persona or pattern from a safe, detached, or observing, point of view.

Descriptions, worksheets, and handouts for of each of these items may be found in the Forum Tools Section starting on Page 47.

Forum Business: A brief moderator-led discussion to cover upcoming calendar items, events, and the like. If a protocol observer was used during the meeting, feedback is given.

Closing: The meeting is closed with quick response questions:

What is your key takeaway or action commitment from today?
What is something or someone you are appreciating here today?
Was there anything done or said that needs to be cleared?
What could have been better today?
What is the **One-Word** you would like to take with you as you re-enter your "real" world?

After the closing, many forums adjourn for a social meal.

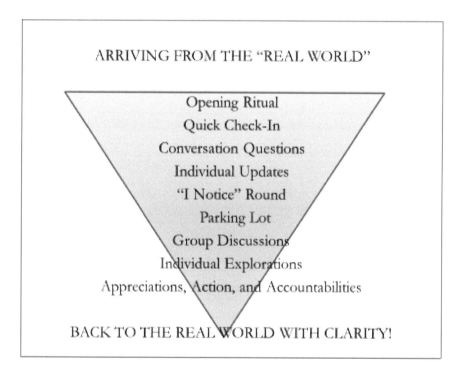

FORUM MEETING AND MODERATOR OBERVATION WORKSHEET
Check all items observed during today's meeting!

	Check	Behavior Observed
1.		Meeting opened on time with an activity that helped the forum break from "real life."
2.		Moderator provided a high level, quick, whole-life check in.
3.		An opportunity was provided to clear the air or disclose anything that might keep anyone from being fully present. Confidentiality was affirmed.
4.		A conversation starter question was asked after the check in and before the update.
5.		The Moderator reinforced that the update is for each member to give airtime to the most meaningful and significant parts of their life. An update form was provided.
6.		**Only the Moderator interrupted updates**. Interventions helped move members along. Observed moderator interventions:
7.		• Endless data: "What makes this significant?" No requests for additional data.
8.		• Endless story: "When you think about all that, what is the underlying emotion?"
9.		• Tears: "I notice your tears. What's coming up for you? How are you feeling?"
10.		• Can't land the plane: "What is it you are really wanting _for yourself_ in this?"
11.		• Bring to completion: "What is your next move?"
12.		Moderator was respectful in managing time and forum protocols. Observed moderator behaviors:
13.		• Said "no" or respectfully stopped any behaviors outside of norms.
14.		• Assisted members in keeping to response times. "Thank you for sharing."
15.		• Re-directed advice-giving by inviting "I statements."
16.		Members provided a reflection or "Notice" after each individual update. Protocols were followed. Observed "noticings":
17.		• Emotion. "When you said, I felt _____", or ""I noticed your <<emotion>>."
18.		• Connection to previous updates: "I noticed ___ was missing from your update."
19.		• Member responses limited to "thank you."
20.		A visual Parking Lot was created. Everyone identified the "one thing."
21.		Within time constraints, Moderator managed the desire for additional sharing. Observed behaviors:
22.		• Additional conversation questions.
23.		• Additional "data" sharing… travelogues, meaningful life moments.

24.		A social break was held with at least some of the time designated as "electronic-free".
25.		Moderator used the break to finalize the second half of the meeting. Observed activities:
26.		• At least one individual explored a meaningful issue or topic using a forum tool.
27.		• A group discussion on a significant topic resulted in individual action commitments.
28.		• Moderator ensured the time was valued and well-used.
29.		• Regardless of tools used, protocols were followed.
30.		Necessary business was conducted in a time efficient manner. Next meeting date was re-affirmed or agreed to.
31.		Moderator provided an opportunity to share learnings, takeaways, appreciations, and "what could have been better?"
32.		Moderator checked to ensure the air was clear after everything that occurred during the meeting.
33.		Moderator provided a closing thought.

What worked well for you in today's meeting?

What could have been better?

What are your personal take-aways or key learnings?

What are you appreciating about Forum?

What is an action you will commit to as you leave today's meeting?

SECTION IV: FORUM TOOLS

"Nine Friends: Maximizing Your Forum" is a constantly evolving and changing toolkit. The following handouts, exercises, and articles comprise the best practices and best thinking of the day. Add to these resources as you maximize your own forum experience!

All worksheets may be downloaded free of charge in 8 ½" by 11" format at www.theprincipalsforum.org.

FORUM OPENINGS

How the meeting opens often sets the tone for your time together. Creating a break from real life is one of the primary benefits of forum. The opening helps us let go of the current worries, thoughts or to-dos.

Forum is often referred to as ritual space. The big idea is that in forum you can try things out, experiment with ideas, feel – and express – your feelings fully in an atmosphere of safety where there are no real world consequences. Only you choose what you take out of the forum experience into your life.

Preparing Members for Forum: Examples of common preparation practices:

- Fall silent. Take 5 long, slow, deep breaths.
- Allow for a silent mediation.
- Use an online guided meditation.
- Visualize the journey for how you arrived in the room. With each step of the visualization, leave that part of the journey behind.
- Imagine all your responsibilities being held in your hands, turn your hands over and let them go.

Preparing the Group: Examples of common group preparation practices:

- Light a candle.
- Read a poem or brief inspirational message.
- Play a piece of music.

 How do we make our forum safe so that each of us can be the first to share deeply?

How do we each best prepare for forum, even while traveling to the meeting?

How do you create a "separation" between forum and the rest of your world so you get the most out of it?

What blocks you from being "all in" for forum?

CONVERSATION ROUNDS

Conversation Rounds are used at the beginning of every meeting. Responding to a thought provoking question after the initial check-in and BEFORE the update helps all members "shift their altitude" and put whatever is happening in life in context with the bigger story. Conversation rounds may also be used when:

- The moderator notices repetitive issues being brought forward and there is a desire to open new levels of communication and connection.
- A few extra minutes in a forum meeting and there is a desire to maximize the use of forum member time.
- New members have joined the forum.
- A forum wants to break the ice after a long break.
- You just want to mix it up a bit!

Process:

1. The moderator selects a question and always responds first to set the tone and time. (See Appendix, Page 126).

2. Members are given a time guideline for response (one to three words, a single sentence, one minute, three minutes)

3. Members have the option to pass once and then be given the opportunity to respond after others have gone.

4. There is no dialogue until all members have responded.

Once all members have responded, the moderator *may choose* (it is not required!) to pose a question aimed at generating additional insight:

What did we have in common? What are our differences?

If you could ask a follow-up question, what would it be?

WELL-BEING INVENTORY AND WORKSHEET INSTRUCTIONS

Use a blank page and draw a four-quadrant template. Consider your assessment of each area of your life.

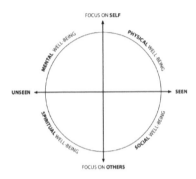

1.   Choose a timeframe ("today" or "this year"). Write words or phrases to indicate your current condition.

2.   Answer the yes/no question, "Is this working for me?"

3.   Identify areas where you desire greater well-being or satisfaction. Complete the Worksheet on the succeeding page.

4.   Finally, congratulate yourself! You've taken the first step toward getting the life you want!

Mental Dimension	Physical Well-Being
The invisible part of you: Values. Principles. Talents. Beliefs. Knowledge. ~How is your mental clarity? What fills your thought life? What do you notice yourself thinking about? ~**Beliefs**: What beliefs are serving you well? Not serving you? What beliefs may want to be challenged? ~**Fear**: How are you experiencing anxiety, making future possibilities real, worrying?	The visible part of you: Self-Care. Use of time. Discipline. Boundaries. Mission. Self-control. ~What is your sense of self-care? The environment in which you live? How is your balance of work, rest, eating, and other activities? ~**Work/Vocation**: How satisfied are you around the challenges, rewards, and your impact in daily life? ~**Anger**: Where do you have crossed-boundaries, injustices, resentments, or giving yourself away?
Spiritual Well-Being	**Social Well-Being**
Your relationship to that which is outside of you and invisible. Connection to your creator and creativity. Wonder and appreciation. Your treasure. Recreation, reflection, and renewal. ~How do you describe your connection to God (or your Creator), and to your most inner self? ~**Purpose**: How clear are you on what it is you were created for? How is your sense of fulfillment? How do you experience your unique creative expression? ~**Joy**: What are your levels of gratitude, reflection, appreciation, recreation, excitement, fun, adventure?	Your relationship to all that is outside of you and visible. Relationships. Touch. Passion. Connection to others in community and in serving the greater good. ~How is your connection to the people most important to you? What is your satisfaction level? ~**Vision**: How are you moving toward a vision for your life, or connected to something bigger than yourself? ~**Sadness/Love**: Where are you experiencing loss, grief, or letting go? How are you accepting love in your life?

WELL-BEING INVENTORY WORKSHEET
AREAS FOR FOCUS AND CHANGE

From your well-being inventory, use this worksheet to identify the key areas where you want a desired future condition that is different from today. An "area" should be as specific as possible ("mental clarity around my family commitments", "physical disciplines for well-being", "connection to my spiritual core"). Think of these as the things you are going to be talking about and focusing upon in the coming months.

Area: Define the specific area you would like to see change.	Current Condition-What are three key data points in this area of your life today?	Thoughts and Feelings: What do you think about the current condition? How do you feel when you think about it?	Desired Future Condition. What will success look life?	Blocks and Risks. What challenges you to action?

MEMBER CHECK IN AND UPDATE WORKSHEET: OPTION #1

<u>Quick Check-In…</u>   <u>Pick one Juicy Word.</u>

Mental Well-Being… Thought life, beliefs, fears.   _____

Physical Well-Being… Self-Care, use of time, work, environment   _____

Spiritual Well-being… Divine connection, gratitude, fun, joy.   _____

Social Well-Being… connection to others, community, a cause.   _____

Shifting Altitude: Conversation Starter

Brief Personal Update
Consider the areas of your life that are significant to you right now. Write three headlines, "tweets", or brief descriptions for the areas that you consider most important.

Area:	Summary:
Area:	Summary:
Area:	Summary:

And then, unpack one with a "story," using this format:

Current Condition ("Just the Facts")	Thoughts and Feelings	Desired Future or "Want"	What Blocks you? What are the risks of action?	Next Steps

MEMBER CHECK IN AND UPDATE WORKSHEET: OPTION #2

Quick Check-In... _____ **Pick one Juicy Word.**

Mental Well-Being... Thought life, beliefs, fears. _____

Physical Well-Being... Self-Care, use of time, work, environment _____

Spiritual Well-being... Divine connection, gratitude, fun, joy. _____

Social Well-Being... connection to others, community, a cause. _____

	What was the "high" point since our last meeting? Why is this significant?	What was the "low" point since our last meeting? Why is this significant?	What's coming up in this area?
Personal			
Vocational			
Relational			
Other			

MEMBER UPDATE: ADDITIONAL OPTIONS

From time to time, the Member Update can be focused on a specific question as opposed to a "whole life" report. Examples:

1. Share about the area of life that has touched your heart, rocked your soul, scrambled your thinking, and/or challenged your strength. What are your next steps?

2. What is going on in your life right now that you have not spoken with anyone about? What are you hiding?

3. If you were to be completely immature and unenlightened right now, what would you have to say about your life? What are you complaining about, blaming others for, or notice yourself playing the villain, victim, or hero?

4. What are you not sharing because you don't want to seem "perfect"?

5. Imagine that it is one year from today. Give a recap of your update from a year ago and an accounting of what has happened since.

The moderator may also define "areas" on the worksheets in different ways. Examples:

1. Pick an area where you are gaining energy, an area that is draining energy, and an area where you are investing energy.

2. Pick an area that you have spoken to no one about/perhaps hiding, an area where you feel blocked or stuck, an area that you keep thinking/talking about but don't act on.

3. Pick an area that is engaging your head, an area that is engaging your heart, and an area that is engaging your gut (or soul).

4. Pick an area in which you have recently resolved or made a decision, an area with at least a one-year horizon view, and an area where you are behind and time is not on your side.

5. Pick an area that seems to be a "repeat" of an old pattern, an area where you are applying a new belief or strategy, and an area where you are curious about the best approach.

6. Pick an area where you are playing the victim, villain or hero, an area where you are in your maturity, and an area where you are unsure about what's really going on.

PARKING LOT WORKSHEET

The "Parking Lot" refers to the inventory of issues that have been "parked" by members for exploration at the current meeting or in the future. Effective forum moderators track the parking lot from one meeting to the next.

Member	Issue to Explore	Urgency (1-low and 4-high)

EXPLORING IN THE RIVER

Exploring in the River invites the forum into the emotional undercurrent with a member on a specific issue, with the presenter guiding the process. Importantly, forum members give up their desire to influence the outcome for the presenting member and instead embrace a posture of self-awareness and listening to their own emotional responses to the presenters' story. One way to think of this is that the whole forum gets in a raft together to explore, with the presenting member at the helm.

The current Condition	It's Not Working!	What is the undercurrent???	What might you let go of?	How do you want to live?

Unpack the Issue: The presenting member takes approximately 10 minutes to unpack the issue with pertinent data, thoughts, and feelings. The moderator may prompt with questions that might include:

- What are the pertinent **facts** that you are responding to?
- What do all these facts mean to you? What is significant? What are the **stories** you are making up around this? What would you think of someone else in this situation?
- Where are you stuck? What have you been unable to figure out? What do you know about yourself, your long-held beliefs, dysfunctions, coping strategies that might be in play?
- When you think about all that how do you feel? What **feelings** are you experiencing right now? Where do you feel it in your body? If your feelings could speak, what would they have to say?
- What is it you say you **want**? What are you willing to let go of to get what you want? What would be the risk of doing that?

This is not a Q&A or coaching session. The big idea is to allow the member to float freely in their story and discover the accompanying emotions and feelings. Invite the member to focus their eyes on a distant wall or object, letting go of any need to perform or "get it right" with the forum.

Group Sharing: During the presenting members' unpacking of the issue, other forum members are listening and connecting to their own reactions and responses. Once the presenter is finished, members are invited to freely share their own emotions, memories and experiences:

Members are invited to focus on their own responses first.

"I noticed my body react when you talked about _____. It felt <<describe the sensation>>."

"I noticed feeling <<emotion>> when you talked about _____."

And then, continuing with:

- "The memory that came up for me was…"
- "Your story really engaged my beliefs around…"
- "The thing I noticed most in me was…"

Examples:

- "When you spoke about your brother's illness, I felt sad. It brought back memories of my dad's decline and passing."
- "When you shared about your business partner, I felt frustratingly angry. It called into question my beliefs around healthy working relationships."
- "I noticed myself getting anxious as you spoke."

The Moderator Checks-In with Value Received: After about ten minutes, the moderator intervenes and asks the presenting member:

- "What is landing for you so far?"
- "What do you want for the remaining time?" This is where the member really takes the lead. Options include:
  - o Continuing with group sharing with perhaps a specific focus.
  - o Request by the Presenter for more in-depth **experience sharing** (not advice giving!) on a certain question or area.
  - o Presenter posing specific questions/going deeper with specific members.

Everyone Shares in the Learning: Once the river has run its course, the exploration closes with:

- Personal sharing by each member on value received or learning. "What I learned about me in this is…"
- Presenter's take away and any action steps.

Exploring in the River Summary

Segment	Approximate Time
Opening: Optional one-word check-in.	0-3 minutes
Member Unpacks the Issue: Member shares pertinent data, story/background, feelings, and desires.	10 minutes
Group Sharing: "When you shared _____, I felt _____. What came up for me was…"	10 minutes
Check in with the Member: How would you like to use the remaining time? • Continuing with group sharing with perhaps a specific focus. • **Experience sharing** (not advice giving!) on a certain question or area. • Presenter posing specific questions/going deeper with specific members.	10 minutes
Learnings and Takeaways: All members share. The presenting member goes last.	10 minutes
Check Out: One sentence closure by each member to give recognition, appreciation, and positive energy. (All)	5 minutes

IN-FORUM EXPLORATIONS: DISCOVERING THE DEEPER WANT

"In-Forum Explorations" give individual members a time and space to air out and explore a disturbing or troublesome issue in their life. In-Forum Explorations are a time of curiosity that:

- Call upon members to engage in thought provoking questions.
- Allow for members to share from their own similar personal experiences.
- Encourage all members to share at a significant level of trust and vulnerability.

In-Forum Explorations are NOT about seeking advice, being told what to do, or turning over responsibility for what is going on to others in the forum. Instead, the format is intentionally designed as a respectful way for forum members to gain value from the collective insight and experience of the forum, without being told how to "fix" their issue.

Opening: If the group is returning from a break, an optional "one word" check-in may be used. The question might be "How are you doing right now?"

Exploration Set-Up: The coach sets the stage for questions and experience-sharing by communicating expectations from forum members (seeking information or alternatives, sharing relevant experiences, "just listening"), and setting boundaries or identifying any obstacles (taboo areas; emotional areas; areas of confusion; safety concerns).

Communication Starter: The purpose here is to launch the exploration, to stimulate thinking, and to break the ice for the presenting member in a way that says "you're not in this alone". A good question is derived by the coach in advance.

- "Describe a time in your life where you felt _____." (Example: "fear" if the presenting member is experiencing "fear")
- "Describe a time when you were at a crossroads in your life and were unsure what to do next."
- "What does it feel like to walk in your shoes right now?"

Responses are brief and the coach always goes first to set the tone. Example:

- "I felt tremendous fear when I was diagnosed with cancer."
- "When my company sold ten years ago I had no idea what to do next."

Coaching Session: A designated exploration coach and the presenter conduct a coaching session in front of the group, but as if they were meeting alone. Think of it as meeting in a "fish bowl" where members are observing. The purpose of the coaching session is to help the presenter clarify the issue, get to the pertinent details, identify the related judgments and emotions, and what it is they want in the issue and from the forum. **Note: If a *pre-planned presentation*, the coaching session may be completed in advance between the coach and the presenter and this step is skipped.**

Presentation by Member: If this is a pre-planned presentation, the presenter describes the nature of the issue (personal, family, business), and the specific facts of the current situation (data- who, what, when, where, why). Once the specific facts are laid out, the presenter provides an assessment of the issue (judgments, opinions, beliefs, implications) as well as any emotions showing up (fears, anger, sadness, joy). Once the current issue has been defined, the presenter defines their "want"- the desired condition or outcome. The presenter describes the options they see to get to the desired condition as well as any preferences.

Though Provoking and Clarifying Questions: Forum members are invited to pose open-ended questions to the presenter aimed at helping the presenter look at the issue from different perspectives. Members may also ask clarifying questions to help decide what pertinent experience they will share.

- "What might the person on the other side of this issue have to say?"
- "Five years from now, what might a home run look like on this issue?"
- "How will you know that you have dealt with this?"

Beware of statements of advice posed as questions: "Have you thought about just firing the guy?" (See "Good Thought Provoking Questions" on Page 93).

Silence: Forum members take one minute to formulate their thoughts and select an experience to share based on the presented issue.

Experience Feedback: Members share pertinent and relevant experiences aimed at providing insight into how members have handled similar situations in their lives. Members know they are sharing from experience when speaking in the first person ("I" or "My") and the past tense ("then"). If speaking in the second person ("you") and the present tense ("now") it is a good chance that advice is being given.

Specific Value Gained: The presenter reflects on what they have heard and gained from the process and from the member experiences shared. The presenter may choose to make commitments to action and accountability at this point.

Forum Member Learning: Each forum member shares what they have learned for themselves from the presentation.

Wrap-Up: Moderator wraps up. If a process observer was assigned, they provide feedback to the forum. If a scribe was used, the notes are given to the presenter. Members give their individual worksheets to the presenter.

Check Out: Each member (with the presenter going last) offers a one sentence closing thought to affirm the presenter, give recognition, show appreciation, and create a positive energy ending.

IN-FORUM EXPLORATION FLOW SUMMARY

Segment	Approximate Time
Opening: Optional one-word check-in.	0-3 minutes
Exploration Set-Up: The Coach summarizes the presenting members' expectations, and reminder for forum members to use worksheet. (Coach)	5 minutes
Communication Starter: A good question to help all members move to a place of empathy. (Coach)	5 minutes
Coaching Session or **Member Presentation of Issue** (Presenter)	10-20 minutes
Thought Provoking and Clarifying Questions to shift perspective as well as assist members in selecting the experience to share. (All)	10 minutes
Silence to ponder what personal sharing is relevant and for members to form thoughts.	1 minute
Experience Feedback (Coach) -Members share experiences and insight -No "you should", "you have to", "we think", generalizing or giving advice -Use "I" or "My" speaking from your head and heart in the past tense	5-20 minutes
Specific Value Gained and Action Steps (Presenter) **-**Define accountability and support	3 minutes
Forum Member Learning (All)	5-10 minutes
Wrap Up (Moderator) -Processor delivers feedback on protocol -Members hand worksheets to presenter -Reminder of confidentiality level	1 minute
Check Out: One sentence closure by each member to give recognition, appreciation, and positive energy. (All)	5 minutes

IN-FORUM EXPLORATION COACHING WORKSHEET
(Coach interviews presenter. Presenter may make notes as desired.)

Name_____Date_____

DATA... JUST THE FACTS! What are the facts related to this issue? Who? What? When? Where? What would the video camera have recorded? What about competing versions of the facts? The other side's view?	
THOUGHTS... WHAT DO YOU MAKE THE FACTS MEAN? What are your thoughts What is your analysis? What is the story you make up about the facts? How are your beliefs or principles informing you? What has kept you from exploring this before? What are the implications of doing nothing? How might someone else view this?	
EMOTIONAL EXPERIENCE What is your primary emotion around this? How is fear at play? What is the bad thing that might happen? The good thing? How are you protecting yourself? From what? What have you lost? What are you letting go of? How have your boundaries been crossed? Where is there injustice?	
WANTS... REQUESTS AND PROPOSALS What options do you see? Do you have a preference? What do you want? If there were no barriers, what would you want? If you had that, what would you really have? What are the future implications to your options? What might the other side want?	
SET-UP What do you want from the forum? What kinds of experiences might members share that would be helpful? How will you know this was a valuable presentation?	
AFTER EXPLORATION IS COMPLETE: CALL TO ACTION What is your new commitment? What are you going to do? Specifically? To whom will you be accountable?	

IN-FORUM EXPLORATION INDIVIDUAL WORKSHEET
(*Worksheet used by individual Forum Members and given to presenter*)

Member Name: _____ Presenter Name: _____

What I see as the presenter's issue:	
What I see as the presenters clear want for themselves:	
My clarifying or thought provoking questions.	
Experiences of mine that align with the presenter's issue and wants.	
MY takeaway: What am I learning about me in this exploration? What action steps might I take?	

THE BRAINSTORMING SESSION

Often, members are clear on their commitment, goal, or "want" surrounding an issue but they may not have clarity on their next steps. This can show up with statements like "I'm not sure what to do here", "I don't see any options", or "I just can't get a handle on this". Forum can offer support in this situation through a brainstorm session. The goal of a brainstorming session is to get ideas flowing, to get unstuck, to get some options on the table. **Brainstorming is not a problem solving or fixing discussion and is best used ONLY when a member is crystal clear on their want or end outcome.** Be on the lookout for "power plays" by members with higher perceived power in the group… sabotaging the value of the session through demands that their idea be implemented or belittling and derogatory comments. Successful forums use brainstorming as a respectful tool to maximize creativity and synergy.

The process:

- Member clarifies the issue, expectations and wants from the Forum.
- Moderator sets a time limit for both the brainstorming and discussion period (i.e., ten minutes to brainstorm and ten minutes to discuss).
- Shift to curiosity: All ideas are welcome. Let go of your need to be right.
- No discussion is allowed until after the brainstorming is concluded. Piggybacking is encouraged (adding or expanding an idea expressed).
- Everyone is welcome to participate, including the presenting Member.
- When the brainstorming time limit is reached, discussion starts with the presenter looking for patterns or themes, asking clarifying questions, and seeking additional input to cull the options.

Good questions from forum during discussion:

- What are the risks of that option?
- What additional data or knowledge might you need?
- How might your emotions play in this issue?
- What might the other side be thinking / planning?

Closing: Each member shares something learned, followed by each member expressing appreciation to the presenting member.

FORUM GENERATIVE DISCUSSION

A generative discussion is one that seeks to "make sense" of a situation and provides an opportunity to explore difficult, polarized, or just different viewpoints and perspectives before determining a course of personal or group action.

If facts are the "what" in a discussion, the generative piece is the "so what?"

Once we have explored the topic, we move to "what next?" in terms of our desired future and possible action steps that will follow. So, think of a generative discussion as the middle ground between *what's going on* and determining *what we will do next*.

When leading a generative discussion:

- Ask a question and then be quiet! It takes time to think. Avoid the temptation to elaborate, explain, or answer the question yourself!
- Encourage broad participation. "What do others think?" "Does anyone have a differing view?"
- Stay curious! When you notice yourself crafting your next statement or defense... take a breath, notice the emotion, and ask yourself... "What's coming up for me?" "Can I let go of needing to be right?"

Make sure everyone is "in": Some discussions might be risky, vulnerable, or exposing. Check to be sure that everyone is ready to engage:

- What might be the risk of exploring this topic?
- What might be the benefit?
- Are we willing to take the risk?
- What long-held beliefs might come into play? What beliefs might we need to put on hold? (Make a list!)

Start with the facts: Start with a presentation of data ("just the facts"). Facts are observable and quantifiable. Facts are not feelings. Facts are not thoughts.

- What has happened? Who? What? When? Where? How Many?
- Is there general agreement on the data?

The next step is to consider questions that help make sense of the data and discover our **thoughts** and beliefs. Pick any of these!

- What do we think?
- What do we make the data mean?
- What "stories" might we make up from this data? How does this data affect our view of the future?
- How does this challenge our values, beliefs, or principles?
- What beliefs do we want to let go of?
- Are there different perspectives?
- How might "the other side" view the data? What might be a polar opposite view>
- What has blocked us from exploring this in the past?
- What can we learn from this data? What are the implications?

And then, uncover the **emotional undercurrent**.

- How do we feel?
- How is fear of the future or the unknown at play?
- How is anger or frustration present? Have any boundaries been crossed?
- What has been lost? What might need to be grieved?
- What might be celebrated? For what are we thankful?

Once the data, thoughts, and feelings have been flushed out, the discussion shifts to **"what do we want?"** Possible questions to pose:

- What do we want to have happen?
- What do we really want? And if we had that, what would we have?
- What do we want that we don't have now?
- What is our request or proposal?
- What is the risk of getting what we want? What might it mean?
- Are we willing to take the risks to gain the possible benefits?
- How do our wants align with our purpose, mission, and vision?
- What might others have to say?
- Where might action or inaction lead to in the future?

Once we discover our **"wants"** from a place of clarity in terms of our thoughts and feelings, we move into the tactical step of **"clean action."**

- How might our wants inform our actions? What will we do?
- What will we do in an ongoing way that will lead to getting what we want?
- What support would be helpful and useful?
- Who will we be accountable to?
- What will success look like?

SUMMARY

Generative discussions can result in individual action steps, or actions to be taken as a group. It can be very helpful at the end of a discussion to share the "mental flow" that has occurred.

> *"The facts are _____. The story I create about the facts is _____, and I feel _____. My want is _____. The action steps I will take are _____ and I will check in with _____ as an accountability partner."*

Close with each member sharing an appreciation or learning.

MEMBER WORKSHEET – GENERATIVE DISCUSSIONS

What is the pertinent data?

-
-
-

What are my thoughts about this?

-
-
-
-

What is my emotional experience?

- I feel _____.

What do I want?

What are the action steps? By when?

1._____

2._____

3._____

HOW IS THAT WORKING FOR YOU?

The pathway to change, growth, and improvement often emerges when you are willing to say… "This isn't working for me!" So, if a forum member is stuck in drama or a never-ending stream of complex complaining or blaming… it might be time to simply ask the question… **"And, how is that working for you?"**

The most common answer is "It's not!" And yet, the behaviors and the dynamics continue to rule the members' life. They figure it out. They continue to find escapes and coping mechanisms. Only when the member is willing to truly say "It's not working!" will this series of questions provide a path to observe the dynamic and determine next steps from a place of maturity.

Communication Starter: The purpose here is to set the stage, to stimulate thinking, and to break the ice for the presenting member in a way that says "you're not in this alone". Each member shares what they are observing in the member and how they see this dynamic in their own life. Examples:

- "I am experiencing you as highly controlling and fearful right now. There is a part of me that is like that and it shows up when I sense I am being attacked or ridiculed and feel fear."

- "My sense of you is that you are stepping in to be the hero in this issue, to fix it, to hold the world on your shoulders. I see that in myself at times too, usually when I'm frustrated that others aren't stepping up."

After all members have responded, the moderator invites the member to the front of the room to work through an inquiry. Members are silent while the member works.

What do you want to have happen? What is it you say you really want for you?

How does it serve you to stay right where you are in this dynamic? (*Might be "keeps me safe", "helps me avoid conflict", "maintains my image", or similar responses*)

How do you "do" this dynamic. What's your part? (*Identify specific behaviors. "Never open up with vulnerability." "Always project that everything is perfect"…*)

What's at risk for you to get what it is you really want? *(Because, if there wasn't some risk, you would have likely gotten this a long time ago).*

Are you willing to take that risk to get what it is you really want? *(Yes or No. If no, then the member forfeits their right to complain about the issue.)*

What are your next steps? *(specific, measurable, attainable, realistic, timely)*

What would support for you look like *(both from within yourself and from others)***?**

What are you learning about you here?

After the member has completed this series of questions in front of the forum, conduct an "I-Notice-Round" (just as in Member Updates) with the member only responding with "Thank You". After completion, invite each member in the forum to share what they are learning about themselves from this time of inquiry.

THE MEMBER "INNER-VIEW"

The Member "Inner View" is a useful tool when it appears that a member is falling into an old pattern or behavior, one that they have identified as a problem or an area of their life that they desire change.

The purpose of the interview, or "inner-view", is to allow the member to engage with this persona or pattern from a safe, detached, or observing, point of view. The member in essence "steps out" of their whole self and into this "inner part" to listen and discover the intentions, desires, and hopes of that part. The process allows the member to become tearful, explosive, dark, giddy, or "in" whatever emotion they are experiencing about an issue identified in their update or while building the parking lot. It is important that the member express the desire and willingly accept the invitation to engage in the process.

Opening: If the group is returning from a break, an optional "one word" check-in may be used. The question might be "How are you doing right now?"

Set-Up: The coach sets the stage by communicating expectations from forum members (active listening, empathy), and setting boundaries and allowing the member to identify any obstacles (taboo areas; emotional areas; areas of confusion; safety concerns).

Phase I: Set-up the interview. Name the part of the member that is showing up in this issue.

- So, as you look at this issue, or when <<this thing>> happens in your life, which part of you jumps into the driver's seat? Who is in charge?
- How would we know that part is showing up? What happens?
- Do you have a name for this part of you? (If the member struggles here, suggest a name "for now" and expect the member to re-name the part later!).
- Would you fully step into this part then so that we can look at your life from that perspective? (Invite member to physically move to a different spot in the room and then close their eyes for a moment to settle in to <<the part>>).

Phase II: Discuss with the "part" its role in the member's life, its noble intention, and honor how it has served the member in the past.

- Hi! Who are you? (Invites member to define the part, speaking in the first person)

- How are you showing up in <*Member's*> life now? How is that working for <*Member*>? How do you think you cause <*Member*> problems?
- When have you shown up before? When did you first show up?
- When did it work for <*Member*> to have you show up? What was going on? (Allow for some story. Who was around? Who wasn't around? How did <*Member*> feel?)
- What might have happened if you hadn't shown up in <*Member's*> life? (Allow this to really "land". And then, honor the noble intention of this part with statements like: "Wow, you really served well"… "Things could have been really crazy if you hadn't shown up"… "I just want to stop for a second and say thank you" …)

Phase III: Discuss with the part what it is that the member wants in their life today and become curious on how this part might be willing to assist.

- So, it sounds like it used to work for you to show up in <*Member's*> life but maybe not now. What are you observing in <*Member's*> life?
- <*Member*> has told me they want something today. What do you think <*Member*> really wants?
- How might you change to help <*Member*> get that?
- What might be the risk of you helping?
- Are you willing to take that risk, knowing what it is that <*Member*> really wants?
- (If "yes") Great! So, is there a feeling, or a word or phrase that you might want <*Member*> to get to remind him that you want to help? (If "no" … go to the next question)
- What would you like to say to <*Member*> on this issue?" (Take notes!)
- Close the interview with an appreciation.

Phase IV: Allow member to step back into their whole self and discuss what was learned in the interview. Recap what the interviewer has just heard and learned from this part, in a way that suggests that the member wasn't really there (Because they weren't! Only a "part" was there!).

- So, we just had a very nice conversation with <<*Persona Name*>> and learned some things that I'd like to share with you… (Focus on the noble intention, and the way in which this part might want to help today). *And then,*
- So, what did you learn from this <*Member*>? (Give a reminder that anytime the "old" persona shows-up, this new way of engaging can be chosen.)

- Is there more?
- Are there any commitments you would like to make, or action steps to take?
- What would support for you look like?

"I notice": Provide an opportunity for Forum members to notice what the interviewed member has just observed, experienced and learned. As in updates, the interviewed member's only response is "thank you."

Forum Member Learning: Each Forum member shares what they may have learned about themselves through the Interview. Where did they see themselves in the member's "part"?

Wrap-Up: Moderator wraps up the process. If a scribe was used, the notes are given to the interviewee.

Check Out: Each member (with the interviewed member going last) offers a one sentence closing thought to affirm the interviewee, give recognition, show appreciation, and create a positive energy ending.

Resource: Ludeman, Kate, and Eddie Erlandson, *Radical Change, Radical Results.* Chicago: Dearborn Trade Publishing, 2003.

WALKING IN TIME

There is much to be drawn from our own journey through different points in time. A "Walk in Time" then is a way to learn from the past as well as gain perspective from the future. Good times to use a walk in time include:

- Launching a new forum
- Welcoming new members
- During individual goal setting or action planning
- Anytime there is a desire to gain greater insight into the current issue

The process is to take a walk through time as if we are there now… using the first person, present tense.

- "I am ten years old and my family just moved to Idaho…"
- "It is one year since I wrestled with that issue at forum…"

Walking in the Past

For walking in the past, pick **one** of these set-up questions:

- "Share 4-5 key moments in your life that contributed to who you are today."
- "Share the highest and lowest moments of your childhood (or vocational path)."
- "Consider the biggest issue in your life today. Share a time in your past where a similar dynamic occurred."

The room is set up with a line down the middle, with various "years" marked off. This can be done with masking tape on the floor. One member is given a specific amount of time (10-15 minutes) to share vignettes. If the member gets stuck at any moment, the moderator may prompt with additional questions… "What does it feel like right now?" or "What's going on around you that seems important?" If the walking member slips into past tense, a gentle reminder from the Moderator is helpful… "Speak to us from that time…"

When completed with the walk, the member sits and the forum completes an "I notice" round… sharing what they have seen and heard using the specific structure:

> "I noticed a ___ year old with _____…"
> "I see a man/woman who…"
> "I noticed your emotion around ___"

The idea in the "I notice" round is to affirm and hear the member. The purpose IS NOT for members to share their own experiences that align with the members', or to share what they think about the member of their story. The presenting members' only response is "Thank you."

When new members are being welcomed, an existing member of the group may do a walk before asking the new member to jump in. Alternatively, all members might be asked to share one vignette or moment as opposed to four or five for the new member.

Walking in the Future

A walk into the future is an opportunity to draw upon our own "future wisdom" for ourselves at this point in time. It is a way to affirm, support, encourage, and guide OURSELVES!

Typically, all members walk into the future together, while working on their own specific current issue or goal. To set up the walk, the coach invites all members to stand on a line marked "today" and write down and then articulate their current issue or goal to the group:

- "My issue is handling the dynamics in my extended family."
- "My issue is creating an authentic team culture in my work."
- "My goal is to have a positive sense of health and well-being."

Next, the coach invites the group to step forward to the next line on the floor and announces the date: "It is three months since we were standing on that line…" Each member is then invited to write their responses in the first person, present tense, to a series of questions:

- What is going on now with the issue you identified ___ months ago?"
- What have you done?
- What have you accomplished?

After writing their reflections, the coach invites the group to step forward to a next line and announces the date: "It is one year since we were standing on that line." Each member is then invited to write their responses to a series of questions:

- "What is going on now with that issue?"

- "What is the significance of the changes made?
- "What is your level of satisfaction?"

This continues for a third round which may be three or five years out. After the third round, the coach invites the group to turn around and while looking at the original line on the floor to respond to the question:

"From this vantage point of _____ years from now, reflect for a moment on where you were and the issues or goals you were facing when you were standing on that line way back when:" And then:

- What feelings do you have for the person facing the issues you identified?"
- How important was the issue?
- What advice do you have for yourself back then?
- What words of support might you bring?

Once completed, each member re-states the current issue to the group and then shares the "words of advice" they have given themselves. Closing questions might include:

- "What are you learning about you in this?"
- "What is your takeaway?"
- "What action steps will you take?"
- "What are you appreciating about this time?"

The tone for "A Walk in Time" is one of reverence, tenderness, and respect. It is not a time for joking and inappropriate humor. Successful forums know that humor used while sharing vulnerable parts of ourselves is a defensive move by the person using the humor and risks shutting the group down from further sharing. Review the handout "When Emotion Shows Up" prior to conducting "A Walk in Time."

LIFE ISSUE DRAWINGS

This drawing exercise allows participants to depict, graphically, the difficult issues they face in their current lives. As in regular updates and the "Walk in Time" exercise, other Forum members give feedback to the participant on what they notice in the drawings.

Three 11 x 17 inch sheets of drawing paper are given to each participant. The participant may select tools (typically crayons or magic markers and sometimes water color paints). Each participant is then given thirty minutes to produce three different drawings:

1) A depiction of their life today

2) A depiction of what they would like their life to look like

3) A depiction of what is blocking them from getting what they want.

Participants are encouraged to use graphical depictions versus words in their drawings. And now the most important part: **the drawings are to be produced using the participant's "off-hand"** (i.e., a right-handed person should draw using their left hand and vice versa) as a way to tap into their more creative, or intuitive side.

When the drawings are completed each participant is invited to share his / her drawing with the Forum. All three drawings are displayed at once. Typically, a participant then takes 5-10 minutes to explain the graphical trilogy. Forum members are then given a couple of minutes to ask clarifying questions about the drawings. Then, the participant is silent while Forum members provide feedback on what they "see" in an individual drawing or the trilogy. For example: "Your spouse is always drawn bigger than you are"; "In your depictions of people, none of them have any faces except…"; "The other people are drawn using varying colors but you always draw yourself in black."

The feedback is meant to mirror what other Forum members see in the drawings. It is not psychoanalysis! The participant can choose to consider or disregard the feedback. As in any exercise where members are exploring their inner world, this exercise must be taken seriously. Often, forum members will be inclined to make humorous or sarcastic comments about potentially sensitive areas shared by the participant. The moderator must be on top of this so that the participant does not feel judged or shamed.

This exercise works best in groups that are serious about going to deeper levels, regardless of the length of time they have met as a group.

SECTION V: FORUM SUPPORT

It is not uncommon, and in fact it should be expected, for issues to surface in any relationship or group. The worst way to resolve an issue is to bury it, ignore it, or hope it will go away. It won't. Unresolved issues and conflict are like festering wounds that often only get uglier with time. And, the ability to keep the air clear, resolve issues, and manage conflict is a skill that grows as relationships develop through speaking and listening using clean communication skills.

Relationships and group life can be likened to paddling a boat or canoe. If everyone has their oars in the water, and paddles according to agreed upon method at the time and with the intensity needed, the boat will make progress. Our experience though is someone, or some group, will at some point have an issue and take their oars out of the water. The primary reasons for this include:

- Lost sense of purpose or goals.
- Confusion on who is making decisions and who is in charge.
- Disregard for agreed upon rules and responsibilities. Hurt or anger around missed expectations.
- Frustration over competing ways to make things work.

Successful forums recognize early warning signs and take immediate action:

- Attendance falling off.
- Use of jokes or inappropriate humor.
- Lack of follow through on commitments.
- Lack of emotion or real connection.

So, what to do?

Awareness of early warning signs is just the first step. From there, take a step back and become curious and ask yourself "How might I be contributing to this issue or conflict?" Or, "How might my efforts to avoid conflict actually be creating it?"

When asked, even people who frequently navigate issues and disagreements say that they would prefer to avoid conflicts. And, we each try to avoid conflict in different ways! Consider the following three primary styles you might use to avoid conflict.

Each style has a benefit, but when used alone has a drawback or possible "mistake" that often *creates* the conflict you are trying to avoid.

Conflict Avoidance Styles

Style	What you might say or think:	How Others May Respond to You:	Try phrases life these:
Take a Positive Outlook	"Let's just always be positive! It's all good!"	"You live in a fantasy world!!"	"We're on the same side." "This can be worked through." "Where are we in agreement?"
Search for Emotional Realness	"Let's connect to our feelings on this. Let's go deep."	"Don't give me your touchy-feely stuff!!"	"Right now, I feel _____." (Scared, worried, disappointed…) I hear you saying you feel _____". Is there more?
Stress Mental Competency and Logic	"Let's just be reasonable here. No reason to get all worked up about this."	"You're sucking the life out of me. You have no feelings. You're always just in your head!"	"I see how I misunderstood things." "What tools do we have to work through this?"

What style do you gravitate to? What style feels unnatural?

Self-awareness about how we are individually wired and the way we respond and react to various situations opens the door to understanding how others in our lives might be different. At our best, we learn to connect to others in a way that creates a win for all. When things start to get heated, a balanced approach to the situation is in order!

And then, as you become more aware you might find yourself moving to a place of curiosity in most every situation! By getting your own feet on the ground, you are in a better position to help others do the same.

Focus on Structure: Agreements and Expectations

Early-detection and response quite often makes the difference between getting back on track and getting stuck in a quagmire of drama, blaming, and complaining. In almost all cases of flagging relational performance, focusing on getting your OARRs back in the water will get things moving forward:

Outcomes	Actions and Agenda	Roles	Rules and Responsibiltiies

"Outcomes": The results we are working toward. Our vision. The destination. When outcomes are unclear, actions often disintegrate into emotional power plays. Effective relationships have a clear vision of hoped for achievement and change.

- "What is the goal here?"
- "Does this action move us toward our desired future?"
- "Can someone clarify where we're headed on this?"

"Actions and Agenda": Our agreements around all the actions we take include schedules, timelines, plans, sequence of events, and processes. These form our expectations of what is going to happen. When expectations are missed, anxiety and frustration surface. Questions like "Who came up with this lousy plan?" begin to set things adrift. Effective relationships allow expressions of feelings of anxiousness or frustration to be expressed *and* are cautious before changing plans based on the emotion of the moment. Relationships benefit from the confidence that whoever is in charge is working from a plan.

- "What's really going on right now?
- "What is the emotional undercurrent?"
- "Where do we have flexibility?"
- "If we change the action plan, what might be the unintended consequences?"
- "Are we willing to trust the process in order to get what we said we wanted?"

"Roles": Everyone has a part in the relationship. In groups, roles are often formalized as "moderator", "chair", or "leader." All group members benefit from understanding their own role and the roles of others.

- "What are our roles in this?
- "Whose decision is this?"
- "What are the concerns here?"
- "Is there an unstated request or proposal?"

"Rules and Responsibilities": In effective relationships, everyone takes 100% responsibility for their part… not 150% and not 50%. Agreements on norms, guidelines, behavior protocols and the like provide a framework for all. Actions that are inconsistent with agreed upon protocols and norms undermine the relationship and reduce the level of trust.

- "What would taking 100% responsibility for my / our part in this look like?"
- "One of our agreements was __. Is that still important to us?"
- "Are we in alignment with our expectations of one another?"
- "An agreement has been broken. How might the broken agreement be repaired?

Focus on Issues with the Group as a Whole

Sometimes, a group falls into habits which inhibit performance or create an environment where performance is compromised. And often, individual group members are reluctant to step forward and "blow the whistle." Group issues show up in different ways and all drain energy from the performance of the group and achievement of desired outcomes. Evidence that the group has fallen into a challenge that needs attention includes:

- Group focuses on problems as opposed to opportunities.
- Group relies solely on the leader for decisions and direction.
- Group relies on experienced members or those with "more power".
- People speak for others. Lack of listening. Inappropriate humor.
- Undisclosed conflicts of interest or competition
- General disregard for guidelines and norms.

What to do?

- Clarify understanding of positive group behavior. "What is going on with us when we're really performing well?"
- Draw out leadership from within the group, especially those who may withdraw or hold back.
- Focus on the basics of group building, especially if new members have joined the group. Ask questions that build safety and trust:
  - What are my wants in this group?
  - What's a part of my story that might be in play here?
  - What might we accomplish if we work together?"
- Create time for group members to clear issues with the whole group using the same format described below for issues between group members.

Focus on Issues Between Individual Members

When two or more members come into conflict- or avoid conflict in the name of group "peace"- the entire group needs to get back on track. You can be sure that there is an issue between group members when you see:

- Misunderstandings or assumptions of others
- Incomplete or unclear communication
- Triangulation (talking to others about another person and issues)
- Personal criticism, untruth, broken agreements

What to do?

In a forum environment, the individuals involved are invited to clear the air in front of the forum. By clearing the air in the group setting, everyone involved gets to grow from the experience and learn that the forum has the strength to work things through. See the sample below as well as the summarized steps.

Focus on Individual Issues

Relationships and group experiences often present challenges which cause us to look inside ourselves and our wiring. This can create emotions and behaviors that work against relational performance. Intervention at this point focuses on allowing the person to experience their own emotions and issues without compromising the integrity of the relationship or the structure that a group must maintain. Examples include:

- Individual shows lack of willingness to give or hear feedback.
- Individual focus is distracted, distanced, withdrawn.
- Beliefs or behaviors which prevent individual from effective participation, including dishonesty, theft, harassment or abuse of self or others.
- Conduct so far off the mark that the individual is putting himself / herself or the group at physical, legal, or other risk.

Real life change happens from the inside out, not the outside in. We cannot force life change. And, the forum experience is not therapy! We can empathize and we can care.

What to do?

- Compassionately clear the air with the member. To avoid "piling on" the moderator may choose to select one member or take it on themselves.
- Allow the member time to reflect on their behaviors and respond if appropriate.
- Show compassion and give encouragement to seek outside help.
- Align the individual with a peer in the forum as an accountability partner.
- Focus on outcomes and expectations. Revisit and recommit to ground rules. Seek agreement on alternative behavior.

We cannot fix an individual. And, we use our best judgment in ending a relationship or removing an individual from a forum when unable to abide by the agreed upon norms, guidelines, expectations, and roles.

Resources: Jim Warner (www.oncourseinternational.com) and Kaley Klemp (www.kaleyklemp.com) have done extensive work with the Issues Clearing Model. Dave Sibbett and his team at Grove Consultants International (www.grove.com) first coined the OARR's acronym back in the day and recognize that it has gone "viral" yet still deserve credit. The National Outdoor Leadership School (www.nols.edu) also uses a "Waterline Model" that follows a similar structure of starting "near the surface" with systems and structure and going deeper as needed. This article first compiled by Vince Corsaro in 2001.

KEEPING THE AIR CLEAR

A simple model for clearing issues between group members involves a one on one discussion (which can be done in front of the group) where the primary expectation is to hear the issue without becoming detoured by defensive behavior. If the issue to be cleared is from an individual to a whole group, the person with the issue selects one member to represent the group by serving as "Person B" in the example below.

Person "A" brings the issue to Person "B" with:

Steps	Example 1	Example 2
Affirm the desired relationship.	"I want to clear this issue with you because I respect you and I truly value our relationship and how we interact with each other."	"I want to get this issue out of the way so that we can get back on the same page, which is where I want to be with you."
A statement of just the **Facts.**	"You arrived at 8:00 for our 7:30 meeting and are usually late"	"I've sent you three e-mails with requests on forum business and not gotten a response"
A statement of **Judgment (or Opinion, Belief, Story)**	"When you arrive late it makes me think I am unimportant and you don't care about me or the other members of the group, and that your own priorities are ahead of ours. I hear you say you're sorry but since the problem continues, I don't believe you or your commitment."	"When you don't respond, I make up a story that you want to make me look bad for some reason. It's like you get some joy out of me scrambling to look good with forum.
A statement of their **Feelings** about the issue.	"When you arrive late I feel angry."	Actually, it's a fear for me. I feel fear that I will look bad not getting done what I said I would do for forum. I also feel mad."

Steps	Example 1	Example 2
A statement of **Ownership**	"I own my part in that I have a hard time believing people."	"I own my part in this that I always want everyone to be happy with me, which is weird because I also own that a part of me wants to be late when we're supposed to meet."
A statement of **Desire or Want**	"First, I wanted to get this off my chest. I also want to hear from you about your level of commitment to this group and your commitment to follow through on your promises."	"First, I wanted to know that you have heard this and are aware of my side. I also want to work out the best way for you and I to communicate."

In many cases, Person "B" tends to craft their defense strategy while "A" is still speaking. This may launch a bunch of excuses, or anger toward "A" about their shortcomings rather than sticking to the issue. Instead, Person "B" makes every effort to **hear** what has been said and follow this structure:

Steps	Example 1	Example 2
Validate the facts to ensure clarity. This is the only thing that needs to be agreed upon.	"I agree that I was a half hour late for the meeting and this is the third meeting in a row when I have been late so it looks like we agree on the facts."	"The facts are that I have received three e-mails from you recently and have not responded."

If there are disagreements on the facts, stop! Even when there are differing versions of the facts, judgments and feelings likely remain. Agree to move forward even though there may be only partial agreement on the facts.

Steps	Example 1	Example 2
Reflect the key feelings, judgments, ownership, and wants. There does not need to be agreement nor a confession of guilt or response. This is designed to ensure the issue has been heard.	"I see that you are angry about this. You believe I am putting other priorities ahead of our meetings and that I am not really committed to the group. You question whether I am sincere when I say I'm sorry. You also own your part in that you have a hard time trusting people. You want to get this off your chest, and you want to hear my commitment both to the group and to be on time for our meetings."	"I hear your anger and your fear that you might look bad in forum not getting your job done. When that happens, you make up a story that I am trying to make you look bad, and that I take joy in seeing you scramble. You own your part that you like to please people and you also see how your being late to our meetings might be in the mix. Your want is for me to be aware of the situation and also want to figure out the best way for us to communicate."
Check for Accuracy	"Did I get that right?"	"Did I get that right?
Check for Completeness	"Is there anything else you want to say about this?"	"Is there any more about this issue?"
Confirm that the Air Is Clear.	"Do you feel understood?"	"Do you feel clear about this? Are you complete?"
Appreciate one another!	B: "I appreciate you for bringing to my attention how much this behavior affected you. I didn't realize it." A: "I appreciate you for listening sincerely and working with me to find a solution that works for both of us."	B: "I appreciate you for sharing this and for how hard you have worked to stay in touch with me." A: "I value our relationship and appreciate you for helping us find a great way to communicate so we can stay in synch."

While Person "A" has been fully heard, Person "B" may realize that they have something to clear. The process resumes with the two parties switching roles.

After the issue is fully clear, the two parties can move on to Conflict Clean-up and seek resolution.

Conflict Clean-up

Once the air has been fully cleared resolution is often worked out between the two individuals. This sometimes takes place in the moment and sometimes occurs outside of the meeting or group setting. Possible routes for conflict clean-up are listed below.

Steps	Example 1	Example 2
Offer and Counter Offer Person B offers a suggestion on resolution; Person A responds with what will work for them	B: "I can be on time if we meet where I work." A: "How about we alternate between that location and another?"	B: "If you text me that you sent me an email, I'll be sure to check and respond." A: " Can I call or text?"
Apologies and Amends Person B offers an apology or asks "How can I make it right"	"What can I do to clean this up with you?"	"How can I repair my relationship with you?"
Discussion of Norms and Agreements	"Let's talk about the norm around punctuality that we have and if / how we want to amend it."	"What agreement do we want to make as a forum about our communication with each other?"

KEEPING THE AIR CLEAR: SUMMARY

Person with the Issue Starts:

"Script"	*Tips*
"I have an issue I'd like to clear with you. Is now a good time?"	*If not now, agree on a time.*
"I am clearing this issue because you – and our relationship – are important to me."	*Affirm the relationship*
"The specific facts are …"	*Recordable data; not judgments*
"My thoughts about this are…"	*In my opinion …; How I perceive this... The story I make up.*
"When I think about this, I feel…"	*Angry, Sad, Joyful, Afraid. Also can be Ashamed, Guilty, Numb, or a physical sensation.*
"My part in this is…"	*Self-aware dysfunctions or patterns that may have helped create or sustain the issue.*
"And, I specifically want…"	*For me. And, us.*

Other person reflects back:

"Let me see if I understand you…"	*Reflect or paraphrase without interpretation with the goal of truly understanding without rebuttal. After reflecting, check for accuracy.*
"Is that accurate?"	*If not, reflect again. Ask for help.*
"Is There More?"	*This is a crucial question. Ask in a kind, genuine, curious, want-to-be-in-relationship voice.*
"Are you clear about this?"	*"Clear" does not mean "resolved" or "fixed". "Clear" indicates "heard". If yes, give an appreciation.*

Switch as necessary. When both parties are clear, clean it up!

Offer and Counter-Offer	*Offer suggestions on how to solve the problem. Counter offer. Agree.*
Apologies and Amends	*Offer meaningful apology or ask "How can I make it right?"*
Discussion on Norms and Agreements	*Agreed upon outcomes, agenda, roles, responsibilities.*

COACHING THE COACH

"A coach is someone who tells you what you don't want to hear, who has you see what you don't want to see, so you can be who you always knew you could be. Tom Landry

"In old Hungary, along the Danube River between Budapest and Vienna, there was a village by the name of Kocs that produced the world's finest horse drawn vehicles. Skilled wheelwrights fashioned these conveyances with spring suspension to comfortably carry royalty over the bumpy river road that connected the two great cities. These carriages borrowed their name from the small township where they were skillfully designed and came to be known as "coaches." And, while the word has grown larger since the first coach rolled out of production in Kocs, the meaning has not changed. A "coach" remains something, or someone, who carries a valued person from where they are to where they want to be. Kevin Hall, "Discovering Your Purpose Through the Power of Words"*

Successful forums encourage all members to hone the skills necessary to coach fellow members through the exploration of issues, emotions, dilemmas, and celebrations. Coaching is not just what happens during an exploration in a meeting! We take a coaching posture with one another throughout our time together. Some thoughts for stepping into the coach role:

- The coach walks "with" and not "for" the member. The coach accompanies the forum mate on THEIR exploration.
- The coach believes that the member is resourceful and whole, capable of taking 100% responsibility for their life choices. It is not up to the coach to have the answers or fix the problem.
- The coach maintains a detached perspective, looking to see a bigger picture. The coach encourages their forum mate to become an observer of their own life.
- The coach welcomes all emotions that might surface without judgment or analysis. "All of you is welcome here."
- The coach provides feedback and insight… "What I see" and "I notice" statements.

While it is possible to coach yourself by taking a step back and considering some different perspectives, inviting coaching from others has a two-sided positive impact: both you and the coach get something valuable which is quite simply, human connection.

Specific duties of the coach in forum:

1. Maintains a clear, detached, objective viewpoint.
2. Provides questions that enable the presenter to explore the data, thoughts, emotions, and desires surrounding the issue at hand.
3. Welcomes emotion with empathy and inquiry. Explores with the member what emotions are surfacing and what support the member wants.
4. Uses good listening skills by reflecting and checking for accuracy.
5. Coaches the presenter on use of clear and clean communication.
   a. Invites member to speak in the first person.
   b. Coaches "not" statements into positively stated language.
   c. Invites member to own their own thoughts, feelings, and wants as simply their own thoughts, feelings, and wants.
   d. Invites member to separate "facts," "feelings," and "fiction."
6. Manages the involvement of forum members. Invites questions. Ensures member questions are clarifying and thought provoking as opposed to advising or probing.

 Describe the worst coach you've ever had. What made them the worst?

Describe the best coach you've ever had in your life. What made them the best?

What are your concerns about stepping into the coaching role?

What are your hopes as a coach?

GOOD COACHING OBSERVATION WORKSHEET
Check the good coaching skills you observe!

Check	Positive Coaching Behavior Observed	Comments/Tips
	Coach looks interested; breathes evenly; demonstrates attentiveness.	
	Coach uses **Open Questions** (those that can't be answered with a single word or yes/no).	
	Coach promotes clear communication with positive language tips.	
	Coach provides a **Reflection** of what the speaker has said (a statement that captures the meaning of what was communicated as opposed to a specific "repeating").	
	Coach checks for accuracy of the **Reflection** ("Is that accurate?")	
	After multiple **Open Questions** and **Reflections**, Coach provides a **Summary** of what has been communicated.	
	Coach checks for additional thoughts or desires ("Is there more?")	
	Coach provides an **Affirmation** or **Appreciation** for the feelings expressed, values, thoughts or desires of the speaker (a specific positive statement delivered with genuine interest)	
	Less Effective Coaching Behaviors Observed	
	Closed Questions (Yes/No or single word answers).	
	"Fix Its" (providing a direct solution or suggestion).	
	"All about me" (Redirecting the conversation to something about the coach).	
	Asking interrogating "why?" questions or getting defensive.	
	Reflections that simply repeat what the speaker said.	
	"Interpretive Responses" that tell the speaker what the listener thinks they mean.	

GOOD THOUGHT PROVOKING QUESTIONS

Members are challenged to ask good thought provoking and clarifying questions of one another. A good question is a powerful way to gain clarity! A good question:

- Shifts the perspective
- Acknowledges emotions in a detached way
- Draws on personal insight and wisdom
- Invites the individual to become an observer of their own life

Less effective questions "lead the witness" to a point of view, cause the responder to defend their position, or are thinly disguised statements of advice. Examples:

- "Have you thought about just firing the guy?"
- "Couldn't your balance sheet handle some more debt?"
- "Don't you think your spouse should know about all this?"
- "Why did you do it that way?"

Most forum members develop their go-to list of thought-provoking questions that can be used at any time. Some favorites:

- How is all that working for you? What do you want to have happen?
- What is the risk of getting what you want? Are you willing to take that risk?
- If you could look back to this moment from five years in the future, what advice would you have for yourself?
- What is the question you don't want to answer right now?
- What beliefs are driving your actions right now?
- What are you hiding? What don't you want us to know?
- If you had no fear, how might you act?
- What is it you really want that you don't have now?
- If you could step outside yourself, what would you have to say about you right now? What do you think of a person in this kind of situation?
- I am not believing you right now. What do you really want to say?

 What are yours?

UN-ENLIGHTENED AND UN-SAFE

"Safety" is a judgment. It is an assessment of a situation. It is a conclusion based on a set of facts. Safety is not a feeling. It is not an emotion. So, when someone says "I don't feel safe here!" what they are really saying is "My judgment is that this place is not safe for me!"

Why is this important? While emotions are simply **the truth of a state of being,** judgments are **changeable**. You can change your judgment of a situation. You can do some things that create a different set of facts and then make a different conclusion.

Our assessment of emotional safety is partially formed by the responses from others. Consider how these responses either contribute to an assessment of safety or detract from it.

A Statement	An unenlightened and unsafe response	A response that promotes safety
"I feel guilty."	"Why do you feel guilty? You haven't done anything wrong!"	"I notice your guilt. It makes sense you might feel guilty. Is there more?"
"We haven't had sex in a month."	"Ha Ha Ha. Look kid, I haven't had sex in a year. Get over it!"	"And, what do you make that mean?"
"I'm not sure what to do."	"Well what I'd do is…"	"What is it you are wanting?"

Most people tend to judge that it is not safe when the listener attempts to fix, explain why emotions are inaccurate or wrong, belittle, or just turn the whole thing around and makes it about them.

 Share a specific moment when you judged that it was unsafe for you to be fully truthful.

Safety is promoted when: the listener avoids making judgment or forming their own point of view about the situation, emotions are reflected, wants clarified, and opinions, thoughts, and suggestions are owned. **What responses would promote safety or detract from safety? What other examples might you have?**

A Statement	An unenlightened and unsafe response	A response that promotes safety
"I'm concerned about the ethics of a key employee and doubt whether I should trust them. I know I am not thinking clearly and would really like the group to just give me some direction. Frankly, if you all just told me what to do I'd be happy."		
"My schedule is completely full and I am just incredibly busy."		
"Last week I wanted to talk about making some vacation plans for next year. When my spouse got home I let them know that I wanted to talk and asked if after dinner would work. They said, no, and that they didn't really want to talk about it for another month or so. I really want to just have a mature and clear conversation."		

 What is our commitment to safety? What do we do when we judge that it is unsafe?

HESITATION TO OPEN UP IN FORUM

Effective forums are on the lookout for members who are withholding or hesitating to share openly in forum. Willingness to become vulnerable requires both a safe environment as well as a commitment to push through stated as well as unknown fears. When a member shares openly, relational trust is the result. Everyone wins.

Moderators noticing hesitation in a member may choose to meet with the member for a conversation:

- "I've noticed that you haven't brought a personal issue to Forum in __ months, and I have been wondering what might be behind that. I have been through stages when I felt hesitant and found that it helped me to speak about concerns, some of which I didn't know I had. Would you be up for a conversation like that?
- Disclose some of your own risks in sharing in forum. Ask if the member is willing to speak about what is at a risk for them to share … or the bad thing that might happen if they share more openly.
- Whatever is said, appreciate the risks. Reflect back with something like, "It makes sense to me that you would not want [the bad thing] to happen. Is there anything I can do to help make sure that doesn't happen?"
- Ask what the member wants from the forum with regard either to this topic, or to his/her overall forum experience.
- Ask: "Would you be willing to take that risk so you could get [the thing you want from forum]?" Accept the answer either way. If yes, ask, "What kinds of things would you be willing to share?" Offer support.
- Suggest the member articulate the risk to the rest of the group in the framing of their presentation.

The Big Idea: In their self-talk, most people make themselves wrong for being cautious about perfectly understandable risks. As a moderator, you invite members to disclose and be appreciated for the risks or concerns they have. This makes it safer for people to share the depth of themselves.

Wants and Risks Exercise Instructions

Use this group exercise with accompanying worksheet to challenge the levels of vulnerability and openness in forum.

1. Written Reflection: On the worksheet, each member writes down the name of each other member in the group, and then completes the two columns:

Wants: What motivates this individual? What do you see as their "big wants" in life? What are they getting from forum when they seem happiest? What is it you see them wanting in their life, or what do you see that gives them a positive outlook?

Risks: What might cause this person to hesitate, to be cautious or to limit their depth of disclosure? What are the things that he or she is protecting themselves from? What are the bad things they don't want to have happen.

2. Sharing Round I: Invite one member into the "hot seat." Each member then shares their specific perceived wants and risks for the member in the hot seat.

3. Personal Reflection: After all members have been in the hot seat, everyone reviews their own notes to consider silently how much what they have written might <u>apply to them personally.</u> Each member considers, "What is at risk for me? What might cause me to hesitate?"

4. Sharing Round II: In this round, each member shares what they see about their own risks and hesitations… as well as their wants. Members are invited to remain curious and challenge their willingness to be vulnerable.

5. Sharing Round III / Assess Willingness to Take the Risk: The final round provides an opportunity for each member to disclose their willingness to risk sharing at greater depth in order to get what they want from forum. And, any answer is acceptable! The purpose here is to put fears and risks into the light and maintain an atmosphere that says all are welcome here.

 What is our forum learning about ourselves and one another?

What is our commitment as a forum?

MEMBER WANTS/RISK WORKSHEET

Member Name	Perceived Wants	Perceived Risks

What is at risk for me? What might cause me to hesitate in being vulnerable?

THE RISK OF CHANGE

If forum members sense difficulty in achieving or sustaining the life they desire, you might do well to consider as a forum what it is you know about the risks and challenges of change. And, the truth is, you know a lot about change, because you live in a constantly changing world.

Individually, make a list of all your long-held beliefs around change and personal growth.

Example: "Change is hard" "I might fail" What else?

_____

_____

_____

Now, let's look at the list.

- Which of these beliefs have served you in the past? Which serve you today?
- Which beliefs might need to be "let go" for you to even explore what you want in your life today? What would be the risk?
- Are you willing to take that risk?

If you are willing to take the risk, then great! If no, congratulations. You have just set a boundary. You have said it is not worth the risk in your life of exploring your deeper wants or how to get what you really want in life today. That's okay. And, in drawing that boundary, you forfeit the right to complain about it. Only when you are ready to take the risks can you step forward in a sustained and life-changing way in any relationship or issue. So, are you willing to take that risk?

THE BIG DEAL ABOUT ADVICE

"You'll find that by coming up with your own solutions, you'll develop a competitive edge.
Maura Ibuka, the co-founder of SONY, said it best:
"You never succeed in technology, business, or anything by following the others."
There's also an old Asian saying that I remind myself of frequently. It goes like this:
"A wise man keeps his own counsel."
Bob Parsons, Founder, Parsons Technology and GoDaddy.com

Use this exercise as a forum discussion topic to clarify the difference between "ADVICE" and "EXPERIENCE".

ADVICE	EXPERIENCE
You know you are giving advice when speaking in the 2nd person: "You" and in the present tense: "Now"	You know you are sharing an experience when you are speaking in the 1st person: "I" and in the past tense: "Then"
Examples:	Examples:
"Here's what you should do…" "If I were you, I would…" "You'd be crazy not to…"	"When ___ happened, I…" "When I did ___, I learned…" "I was crazy when I ___"

Let's Play Point-Counter Point

1. Pick a side. "Give Advice" or "Share Only Experience".
2. Build your argument why the side you picked is the right side.
3. Present your argument to the group. Listen to the other side.
4. Craft your Response to the other side's argument.
5. Present your responses to the group.
6. What have you learned?

What is our desire in forum?

When is advice-giving okay?

ACTION AND ACCOUNTABILITY
Being an effective "Accountability Partner"

In the past you may have looked at accountability as something done to you. Someone held you accountable. Today, in your commitment to take 100% responsibility for all the results you are getting in life, you may want to think of accountability as something you hold yourself to. You choose to hold yourself accountable.

Whether a friend, forum mate, or peer, you can choose an accountability partner. Effective accountability partners care about your success but are not intertwined in your success... no employees, spouses, or kids! The Accountability Partner role is to come alongside you and commit to these underlying principles with you:

1. You are taking 100% responsibility for the results you are getting in your life.
2. You are desiring a safe place to account for your actions toward getting what it is you want in your life. In a way, you are asking your accountability partner to hear your immaturities as you seek to live in your own maturity. It is your job to speak. It is your accountability partner's job to listen and reflect what is being heard.
3. You are resourceful and whole. You are determining the best solutions and strategies for your life. Your accountability partner is accompanying you on your journey... walking with you, not for you.

Effective accountability partnerships make scheduled time commitments and are rooted in good questions.

What Happened? Always Start with the Facts!
What did you do that you said you were going to do?
What did you do that you said you were not going to do?
What did you not do that you said you were going to do?

Making Sense of What Happened:
What did you learn?
What is your level of satisfaction?
What worked well? What could have been better?
What was going on inside of you before, during, or afterwards?
What was your emotional experience then, and now?
Where did you notice sabotaging or self-betrayal? Self-criticism? Immaturity?
What are you hiding? What are you not believing?
What are you appreciating about you?

Next Steps

What is still important to you?
What do you want to have happen next?
What might you want to let go of?
What beliefs might want to be challenged?
What agreements need to be repaired, re-affirmed, or re-negotiated?
What is your commitment to yourself?
What is your plan?

When your accountability partner wants to fix, solve, or give advice, ask them… "What experience have you had that compels you to give me that solution?"

WHEN EMOTION SHOWS UP

Sadly, true emotions are not often welcome in many groups and our culture often works hard at eliminating emotion from our lives.

What you may have been taught:	What it means:
"Boys don't cry."	The emotion of sadness is not acceptable.
"Girls are always polite."	The emotion of anger is not acceptable.
"There is no place for emotion in the workplace."	Who you are really isn't welcome.

Emotions simply are. "I feel sad." "I feel angry." "I feel afraid." "I feel joyful." There is no positive or negative judgment necessary. As we learn to experience our emotions, we can be conscious in our choice of how to respond in that emotion. Being angry is not a bad thing. Hitting someone over the head with a baseball bat is. Emotions are like waves that wash over us on the shoreline. They come in and they go out.

Often when emotion shows up someone in the group will offer a tissue or everyone looks away. Or, immediately someone moves to "fix" the emotion... "Oh, don't be mad!" Or, "It's okay, no need to cry..."

Effective forums allow and embrace emotion, because there is an understanding that emotions are signaling some truth in our life at that moment. So, if at any time during a forum meeting emotion shows up, STOP! Never negotiate with emotion, or continue with tactical work when emotions are potentially "driving the bus". Be on the lookout for any emotion showing up, including:

Fear	Anger
Anxiety, guilt, worry, or confusion due to the unknown or possible outcomes. Often shows up in the gut, as a headache, increased breathing or heart rate, general unease.	Frustration, irritation, disappointment, or desire for revenge due to any boundary being crossed, betrayal, or other cause. Often shows up as tightness in the neck or shoulders, a clinched jaw, head pain
Joy	**Sadness**
Aliveness, tenderness, compassion, excitement, or gratitude surrounding an issue or event. Often shows up as a tingling all-over feeling, tears, pleasure in breathing deeply.	Down, distraught, grieving, lost or letting go due to some loss. Often shows up through tears, slumped shoulders, heavy sighs.

Instead of ignoring or fixing the emotion, shift to curiosity and genuine empathy. Mirror the "energy" of the member (i.e., quiet, aggressive, tender, sharp). Stay until the person is complete.

Good questions to ask include:

- I notice your tears. What are the tears about? What are they meaning?
- I notice your facial expression isn't matching your words. What's really going on?
- What's coming up for you right now?
- *Mirror the emotion:* I see that you are feeling _____.
- *Honor appropriately:* It makes sense that you might be feeling _____ right now.
- Is there more?
- What do you want right now?

When emotion is welcomed and embraced, it almost immediately begins to dissipate. Like the wave going out. And then, we continue in a more connected and holistic way.

Successful forums allow members to experience emotion and talk openly about their emotional experience.

 What have we noticed about our responses when emotion shows up?

How would we like to be as a forum in this area?

SECTION VI: PERSONAL GROWTH IN FORUM

Most forum members are committed to an ongoing process of learning and development as well as a pursuit of meaning and purpose in their lives. The following exercises provide a starting point for both individual work and forum conversation. These may be used on retreats, as conversation starters, or generative discussions.

Purpose/Principles/Mission/Vision

Planning for Well-Being

PURPOSE / PRINCIPLES / MISSION / VISION

"The unexamined life is not worth living"
~*Socrates*

The following exercises allow forum members to explore some of the bigger questions of life. These exercises are often best done on a retreat or extended meeting. They can also be worked on individually and reported back to the forum.

The big idea is to get clear on four key statements for your life:

Your **PURPOSE**, your reason for being, is likely given by others... by your creator, your ancestors and forefathers, or even your parents. This is your WHY. When clear, your purpose is often simple and easy enough to be distilled down to a sentence that can be read in one "outbreath" and understood by a 12-year old! Think of purpose as WHO you are before you do anything.":

Your **PRINCIPLES** guide your life and become the filter through which all decisions pass. These might be beliefs or "things you hold to be true" about the human condition or civil society, character traits you value, or the rules you live by. Principles define HOW you roll.

Some would say that your **MISSION** is defined as "what you cannot not do." You know you are aligned with your mission when you are "in the zone", at your best, performing almost effortlessly. And, you may have never expressed your personal mission. Your mission is a choice. You determine WHAT it is you will do with the gifts, talents, skills, abilities, attributes, and wisdom in your life.

Your **VISION** defines WHERE it is you desire to go in this life. It gives direction and helps avoid wandering aimlessly as you do what it is you choose to do. Vision also defines how the world will be different because you were here. Some say that your vision, or your passion for a different or better world, comes from your greatest pain.

As you gain clarity on these four guiding statements, the task of setting measurable goals and strategies for success falls into place.

Enjoy the journey!

PURPOSEFUL CONVERSATIONS

*"Mission, vision, vocation, calling, bliss, meaning, passion—these
are just some of the words that have been used to describe our
human need to identify and express purpose. Ultimately, finding
your purpose is a spiritual quest. It represents your ability to
connect with something greater than yourself."*

"Finding Your Purpose-A Guide to Personal Fulfillment", Barbara J. Braham

What is your deeper purpose? Perhaps, you have a sense that your life is bigger than you are currently living. Perhaps you are so consumed with "doing" life that you have forgotten what it means to "be" you?

One way to connect with your essence and your joy is to play. Here, the purpose is to express your creativity and do something that "re-creates" you. Creative cooking, sports, intimate sex, and engaging in our own creative arts often leave us saying "It's great to be alive!" Another way to discover your essence is to get quiet and reflect. Listen to the small still voice inside that always seems to know your deeper needs and desires. Do both!

What nurtures you? Brainstorm a list of the things that nurture you. These might be places, activities, and the presence of specific others. For example: "Sitting on a rock by a beautiful lake" or "Skiing a mogul run from top to bottom" or "Eating a donut with my favorite aunt."

_____

_____

_____

What is unique about you? What makes your wiring different than others? What are those positive attributes that make you, you?

_____

_____

_____

Complete the sentence, "I am…" with all the roles that you assume and play in your life. For example, "I am Mom." "I am an Executive."

I Am_____

I Am_____

I Am _____

After completing the list, reflect on the following question: "Who am I if all of the roles that I play are taken away?"

_____

_____

_____

Create a working sentence for defining your life's purpose. This doesn't have to "stick" forever, but what is your sense today?

_____

_____

_____

THE RAILS FOR LIFE: GUIDING PRINCIPLES

Before you begin fulfilling your life purpose, it is essential to ask yourself, "What is most important to me *how* I live my life?" The process of reflection and ranking helps you become more aware of yourself as a person with a choice about your destiny. Awareness about what is important to you gives you the framework and freedom to choose specific endeavors, associations and lifestyle that help you express that which is important to you. With awareness, you can also assess whether you are allocating time and resources to the enhancement and development of that which you value.

1.   Circle the five keywords below that are most important to you. Revise or replace any of the words with a word or short phrase that works better for you.

Family	Health	Learning
Leisure	Relationships	Fulfillment
Financial Success	Privacy	Sense of Purpose
Play	Recognition	Advancement
Security	Companionship	Challenge
Appearances	Friendship	Being Responsible
Personal Development	Honesty	Sexuality
Professional Growth	Creativity	Self-esteem
Spirituality	Integrity	Comfort
Self-Expression	Winning	Connection
Developing Others	Vulnerability	Caring
Physical Touch	Caring	Leadership
Surroundings	Physical Environment	Friendship
Independence	Leadership	
Community	Respect	

2. Review and reflect on your choices.

3. Prioritize the words in rank order. By ranking, you are not saying that any of these are unimportant; you are saying that other things are more important.

4. List your five words in prioritized order in the space provided below. Further clarify your keywords by writing terms that you associate with each of the top five you selected.

Example:
Keyword: PHYSICAL ENVIRONMENT
Associated words: NATURE, BEAUTY, ORDER, COMFORT, and FREEDOM.

	Key Word	Associated Words
1		
2		
3		
4		
5		

These keywords become the principles that guide your life. These words help you make decisions on whether you will go left or right, buy or not buy, go or not go. They begin to help you make choices and describe **HOW** you live… How you roll.

Now, take your keywords and craft a sentence to create "Guiding Principles" for your life. You might start the sentence with "I desire to live in a way that…" This doesn't have to "stick" forever, but what is important to you today?

_____

_____

YOUR STORY

Your story is yours. No one has lived your story except for you. Your story forms your identity. It forms your beliefs. Your story includes heartache and sorrow, joy and gratitude, anger and frustration, risks avoided and fears faced.

What is it you are passionate about? Where did that passion come from? What was going on in your life when you learned about it?

How have you come to terms with your story—the un-filtered, un-edited, un-airbrushed truth of your life?

One way to connect with your story is to tell it! To identify the characters (all the villains, heroes, and victims) who have played their roles and left a mark on you. There is no shame in your story. You are human.

As you read this, you might be asking: "But I've had a wonderful life! Why give attention to the painful parts?" Thanks for asking! What is your sense on that?

Allow yourself to reflect on your story. Perhaps you will discover some things about yourself that you didn't know. Perhaps you will connect to a deeper sense of vision for what you hope to create in the world for yourself and others.

1. Spend some time and **write your story**. You might focus on the times in your life that you learned some truth about yourself. You might focus on the most joyful moments and the most painful moments. And, remember, the "data" of what was going on is less important than the lesson learned.

2. **Imagine that you are able to be an observer at your own funeral. What will your loved ones say about the difference you made in their lives? In the world?**

_____

_____

_____

3. If there were five things you could pass on to the next generation, what would they be?

1.
2.
3.
4.
5.

4. As you look at your life story and the experiences that have shaped you, what are the things that you learned about you that perhaps weren't really true? What might you want to change?

So, as you reflect on your story and all that makes you uniquely you, <u>what difference do you hope to make in the world for yourself and others</u>? What is your vision for your life?

_____

_____

_____

_____

_____

_____

YOUR DEEPER WANTS

A transformational moment often occurs when you discover what you *really* want. Because, when you know what you want, you begin to become it. You change.

Transformation occurs when you clarify your desires in light of the current reality of your life, and in alignment with your deeper purpose, your sense of vision, and the things you value and truly believe. Transformation gives life to your mission. It is a choice you make.

And, there is risk in stating your deeper wants. You may have been conditioned in your life to soften or hide your "want" out of the belief that you would never get it. These include inner dialogues like you weren't important enough, or that others might not value what you want.

"OUR DEEPEST FEAR is not that we are inadequate. Our deepest fear is that we are powerful beyond measure. It is our light, not our darkness, that frightens us. We ask ourselves, who am I to be brilliant, gorgeous, talented and fabulous? Actually, who are you not to be? You are a child of God. Your playing small doesn't serve the world.

There's nothing enlightened about shrinking so that other people won't feel insecure around you. We were born to manifest the glory of God within us. It's not just in some of us; it's in everyone.

And as we let our own light shine, we unconsciously give other people permission to do the same. As we are liberated from our own fear, our presence automatically liberates others."
-Nelson Mandella in his 1994 Inaugural speech as President of South Africa

As you become clear on your deeper wants, you also gain clarity on your personal mission. Some would say that your mission is defined as "what you cannot not do." You know you are aligned with your mission when you are "in the zone", at your best, performing almost effortlessly. And, you may have never expressed your personal mission. As you reflect on these questions, consider that your mission is a choice. You determine what it is you will do with the gifts, talents, skills, abilities, attributes, and wisdom in your life.

Think of the times in your life when you were at your best. What was going on? What were you particularly proud of?

_____

_____

_____

If you could do anything, and if you had all the money you needed, what might you do?

_____

_____

And finally, answer for yourself:

My deeper want for me and my world is_____

_____

And I will bring this want to life though my life mission, to:

_____

_____

PLANNING FOR SUCCESS

Clearly knowing what you want leads to clean and decisive action. And, your chances of success increase when your wants are aligned with your purpose, principles, mission, and vision. Summarize these statements for yourself based on the work you have completed so far:

My Purpose is to be _____

_____

My Mission is to _____

_____

The Principles that will guide me are_____

_____

And, the ultimate difference I hope to make, my vision, is to_____

_____

_____

Goals or outcomes are statements that define success. Goals are often measurable, have a time horizon for achievement, and are often based on some commitment you have made to your best self. Goals are not "action statements" but drivers for future action that will result in achieving a desired future. Examples:

- *Increase my net worth by 10%.*
- *Maintain medical indicators of good health and body weight at +/- 190.*
- *Complete my home renovation project.*
- *Engage in 25 significant mentor relationships.*

Commitments are agreements you make with yourself to define a way of living. Commitments are directed toward your goals and desired outcomes. Examples:

- *I am committed to self-care, physically and environmentally.*
- *I am committed to authentic relationships with myself and others.*
- *I am committed to curiosity and ongoing learning.*
- *I am committed to adventure, creativity, and fun.*

Strategies are the things you do in an ongoing way that move you toward achievement of your goals. Strategies align with your commitments to a way of living and imply choice: you choose a strategy among options. Good strategies help you say "no" to some actions and "yes" to others. Strategies related to well-being commitments might include:

Physical Well-Being
- Eat and sleep well
- Move every day
- Maintain home environment that is light, clean, and nurturing.
- Engage in work that is motivating and satisfying.

Mental Well-Being
- Read for pleasure and learning
- Challenge long-held beliefs
- Name fears when noticed
- Seek knowledge

Spiritual Well-Being
- Quiet prayer/meditation daily
- Create art, food, or music
- Engage in enjoyable activities
- Express appreciation and gratitude

Social Well-Being
- Connect with a loved one
- Connect with a small group or community
- Be of service
- Acknowledge and express emotions

No one can do all things all the time. So, you get to pick. On the next page, select 12 strategies for daily living that will move you toward the well-being goals you have defined. You may change strategies any time you notice that a strategy isn't working for you!

THE DAILY DOZEN

Identify 12 strategies that you believe will best contribute to your sense of well-being. Track the strategies that you act upon and then assess your overall sense of well-being for the day. Take time to reflect on what you are learning about you!

Area	Strategy	Day 1	Day 2	Day 3	Day 4	Day 5	Day 6	Day 7
Mental Well-Being								
Physical Well-Being								
Spiritual Well-Being								
Social Well-Being								
	Number of well-being strategies acted upon today							
	Overall sense of well-being today (1 low and 10 high)							

SYSTEMS AND STRUCTURES

Effective and efficient actions are the result of thoughtful goals and strategies that are aligned with your deeper purposes and wants. Every step you take is a choice, and thoughtful planning helps you make action choices that align with the best life you want to create!

As you reflect on the goals and strategies you have defined, ask yourself:

What drains energy from me? What am I tolerating in my life?

We all have annoyances that we just put up with because we don't want to take the time or energy to make changes. And, sometimes, it is crazy to think that you can make significant improvements in your well-being without making some changes. So, where are some areas that you are tolerating in your life? These can be very simple things like "I have nowhere to sit and read in my home." Or, "my car is constantly filthy."

_____

_____

_____

In order then to get what you want in life, what systems or structure might need to change?

"Structures" are the material things you put in place to support well-being. For example, if a well-being strategy is to ride your bike daily, but you don't own a bike, a new structure for you will be to acquire a bike and helmet, have a place to safely store it, perhaps learn about maintenance and care, and the like. Another structure for social well-being might be to pick a coffee spot and regular meeting time, and let the friends you'd like to connect with know that you'll be there and invite them to join you. Other examples:

Environmental Structures: Refresh home-office spaces, garden plots, lighting and furniture to optimize reading and journaling, or engage in community projects to refresh parks or playgrounds.

Activity Structures: Acquire equipment necessary for desired activities, create or join a group of others with similar interest, learn a new skill.

Support Structures: Engage with a mental health professional, physical therapist, or support group.

Lifestyle Structures: Bedding that is easy to make up. Clothes that are fresh and stylish for you. Water purifiers. Good sunglasses.

Financial Structures: Appropriate bank accounts to support well-being desires for savings and future planning. Cutting up unnecessary credit cards. Starting a side-business to enhance income or pursue a creative desire.

So, ask yourself, "What might be some new structures that will support my goals and strategies for well-being and reduce the areas I am tolerating in my life?"

_____

_____

_____

"Systems" are ways of doing things. So, if a well-being strategy is to "eat well", you might want to consider a system of recording your daily eating habits. This might be an app on your smart phone, an excel sheet, or a hand-written journal. Another system might be the way you shop for groceries. You might want to create a system of shopping every other day for fresh foods and only weekly for non-fresh foods. Other examples of systems:

Home Management: Systems to de-clutter your environment (closet organizers, storage containers, removal of un-necessary junk), maximizing technology for calendars and planning,

Financial Management: Conversion to non-paper bills, electronic bill payment systems, online recording of budget and expenses to track progress.

Lifestyle Management: Shopping list systems that reinforce healthy eating desires and minimize waste, joining small groups that support well-being, personal journaling.

So, ask yourself, "What might be some new <u>systems </u>that will support my goals and strategies for well-being and reduce the areas I am tolerating in my life?"

_____

_____

_____

_____

LONG HELD BELIEFS

Beliefs include all the stories about yourself that you've picked up over a lifetime. And sometimes, long-held beliefs no longer serve you! And even better, sometimes long-held beliefs about yourself were never true in the first place!

So, an area of change for you might be to let go of a long-held belief and adopt a new belief. For example, you may carry a belief that "I am no good at setting and staying committed to goals." As you reflect on your life, you might discover that you've likely kept jobs, shown up for work, completed projects, or done any number of things that you set out to do! So, reinforce the optimism of your belief about yourself. "In the past, I have believed that I was no good at keeping to goals. Upon reflection of my life today, I am believing that I have the ability to set goals and stick to them." And then, build your action plan under this new belief!

Begin to list beliefs that you have about yourself and your ability to change and grow. This list will constantly change and grow!

_____
_____
_____

Now, let's look at the list again.

- Which of these beliefs have served you in the past? Which serve you today?

- Which beliefs might need to be "let go" in order for you to go after what you are wanting in your life?

- Are you willing to take that risk?

If yes, then great! If no, congratulations. You have just set a boundary. You have said it is not worth the risk in your life of going after what you really want in life today. That's okay. And, in drawing that boundary, you forfeit the right to complain about not having what it is you think you might want in your life. Only when you are ready to take the risks of exploration can you step forward in a sustained and life-changing way. So, are you willing to take that risk? If so, you might make some statements like these:

_In the past, I have believed _____, and I now see _____. Today, I choose to release that belief and replace it with the belief_

_____.

ACTION PLANNING WORKSHEET
Reproduce this worksheet in your journal or a document on your computer.

What <u>Structures, Systems, Beliefs, or Way of Living</u> do you want to change?

_____

1.   What is the big measurable goal that this change will move you toward?

2.   What is the key strategy or ongoing commitment that is driving these action steps?

3.   What risks have you determined you are willing to take to make this change?

4.   What will you get from this change? What wants will be fulfilled?

5.   How will you know that you have achieved this desired change?

Specific, Measurable and Observable Action Steps

1.   _____By When _____

2.   _____By When_____

3.   _____By When_____

Who will you hold yourself accountable to on completion of each action step?   (Best if an objective voice and not an employee, spouse or child).

APPENDIX

FORUM OPENING THOUGHTS

Let Your Light Shine (Marianne Williamson)
"Our deepest fear is not that we are inadequate. Our deepest fear is that we are powerful beyond measure. It is our light, not our darkness that frightens us. We ask ourselves, who am I to be brilliant, gorgeous, talented and fabulous? Actually, who are you not to be? You are a child of God. Your playing small doesn't serve the world.

There's nothing enlightened about shrinking so that other people won't feel insecure around you. We were born to manifest the glory of God within us. It's not just in some of us; it's in everyone.

And as we let our own light shine, we unconsciously give other people permission to do the same. As we are liberated from our own fear, our presence automatically liberates others."

Risk
To laugh is to risk appearing the fool.
To weep is to risk appearing sentimental.
To reach out to another is to risk involvement.
To explore feelings is to risk exposing our true self.
To place our ideas, our dreams, before the crowd is to risk loss.
To love is to risk not being loved in return.
To live is to risk dying.
To hope is to risk despair.
To try at all is to risk failure.

But to risk we must,
Because the greatest hazard in life is to risk nothing.
The man, the woman, who risks nothing,
  does nothing, has nothing, is nothing.

They may avoid suffering and sorrow, but they
cannot learn, feel, change, grow, love, live.
Only a person who risks is free.

Taught to Fly
When we come to the edge
Of all the light we have
And we must take a step into
The darkness of the unknown,

We must believe one of two things:
Either we will find something firm to stand on
Or we will be taught to fly.

A Prayer

"Lord, make me an instrument of thy peace. Where there is hatred, let me sow love, where there is injury, pardon; whence here is doubt, faith; where there is despair, hope; where there is darkness, light; and where there is sickness, joy. O Divine Master, grant that I may not so much seek to be consoled as to console; to be understood as to understand; to be loved as to love, For it is in giving that we receive; it is in pardoning that we are pardoned; and it is in dying that we are born to eternal life."
--St. Francis of Assisi

Inspirational Quotes

"From this hour I ordain myself loos'd of limits and imaginary lines.
Going where I list, my own master total and absolute. Listening to others, considering well what they say, pausing, searching, receiving, contemplating.
Gently, but with undeniable will divesting myself of the holds that would hold me."
--Walt Whitman, "Song of the Open Road"

"One of the illusions of life is that the present hour is not the critical, decisive hour. Write it on your heart that every day is the best day of the year. He only is rich who owns the day, and no one owns the day who allows it to be invaded with worry, fret, and anxiety. Finish every day, and be done with it. You have done what you could."
--Ralph Waldo Emerson

"Too many of us become enraged because we have to bear the shortcomings of others. We should remember that not one of us is perfect, and that others see our defects as obviously as we see theirs. We forget too often to look at ourselves through the eyes of our friends. Let us, therefore, bear the shortcomings of each other for the ultimate benefit of everyone."
--Abraham Lincoln

"Our task now is not to fix the blame for the past, but to fix the course for the future."
--John F. Kennedy

"People say that what we are all seeking is a meaning for life. I don't think this is what we're really seeking. I think that we're seeking is an experience of being alive."
--Joseph Campbell

"Every day is an opportunity to make a new happy ending. May you live all the days of your life."
--Jonathan Swift

"Climb the mountains and get their good tidings. Nature's peace will flow into you as the sunshine flows into trees. The winds will blow their own freshness into you and the storms their energy while cares drop off like autumn leaves."
--John Muir

FORUM DISCUSSION AND CONVERSATION STARTERS

Member Background and History
- What is your most significant memory from your teenage (or elementary age) years?
- When you were a child, what did your parents want you to be when you grew up?
- What was your first job? What do you remember most about it?
- Describe a time when your life changed dramatically as the result of some random influence or event.
- Describe an important life decision you made primarily on gut feel or intuition.
- Describe the 2-3 biggest decisions you have made in your life.
- How many do you have of each: mentors or coaches, close friends whom you can be vulnerable with, protégés whom you coach?
- I have found the most meaning in my life from _____.
- What one line would you like to have written on your tombstone?
- What unanswered questions do you have that you would like your Higher Power to answer?
- What, if anything, would you be willing to die for?
- Which holiday has the most meaning for you? Why?

Life Purpose
- What nurtures you? Brainstorm a list of the things that nurture you. These might be places, activities, the presence of specific others.
- What is unique about you? What makes your wiring different than others? What are those positive attributes that make you... you?
- Complete the sentence, "I am _____" with the roles that you assume. For example, "I am Dad." After completing the list, reflect on the question... "Who am I if you take away all of the roles that I play?"
- When we are aligned with our "deepest wants" it is likely we are touching our essential purpose. When do you feel most "in the zone", most alive, most "you"?

Joy / Gratitude
- What are a couple of things you remember (fondly) about your parents or grandparents?
- When you were a child, what did you want to be when you grew up?
- Describe one of the greatest adventures you have ever been on.
- Do you think you are "lucky"? Why or why not?
- I believe that you (member name) are really good at _____.
- Talk about 2-3 things you really enjoy and do very well.
- What is the one thing you like best about yourself?
- What day of your life would you most like to re-live? Why?

- What has been the best year of your life?
- What is the one compliment you most enjoy hearing from someone close to you? From a stranger?
- What was your greatest learning in the last year?
- You have three wishes… what would you wish for?
- You have been granted one hour with the President of the United States when you will have his/her undivided attention. What would you ask him or tell him (or her)?
- Describe one of your teachers who made a big impression on you.
- What one person has done the most to make you who you are today? Describe his or her impact.
- Who either have been or currently are the top 2-3 mentors in your life? Why?
- For what in your life do you feel most grateful?
- What would you rate as your single highest achievement?
- What is the best part of achieving your goals?
- Describe a time in your life when you felt you had boundless energy.
- If you could have a personal board of directors, consisting of up to three people living or dead, whom would you want on your board?
- If you could have world-class skill in any single field, what would it be? Whom would you want to know that you have this skill?
- What, if anything, do you do so well, and enjoy so much, that you would consider making it your vocation without pay?
- Who was the best boss you ever had? What made him or her so good?
- Who was your hero as you were growing up? Who is your hero today? How did/do you try to imitate him or her?
- Describe a friendship that has lasted more than ten years. Which of your current friends will be important to you ten years from now?
- Who is the most important person in your life? What could you do to improve the relationship?
- What is the one sentence legacy you would like to leave mankind?
- Talk about someone you know who really seems to have their life together. In particular, what do you admire about his or her life?
- Describe one very good decision you have made. What factors in making your decision contributed to its success?

Life Principles
- In your view, what are the rails, the virtues, the inarguable behaviors necessary for a civilized society? How do you see the world "stacking up" today? Where are we out of alignment?
- When do you notice yourself "out of integrity" with who you are? What's going on? What is it you are really wanting in that moment?

- When do you become most critical of yourself? What is the message you receive? What is going on?
- What beliefs of yours have changed since your 20's? 30's? 40's?
- What are the important things for you to "keep in mind" as you plot the next twenty years of your life?

Anger / Action
- Describe the circumstance around the last time you were in a fight. What caused it? Who won?
- Have you ever been stung by the betrayal of a close friend? How has the experience affected your other relationships?
- What steps do you need to take, immediately, for the next stage of your life to be better than the last?
- Describe the last time you didn't have the guts to say "no".
- What boundary is the hardest for you to enforce?
- What do you let others "get away with" – that isn't really ok with you? How do you feel during? After?
- What do you feel resentful about?
- I stand for _____.
- If you opened your mailbox to find a check made out to you for 10 times what you will earn this year, what would you do? What if it was 100 times what you will earn this year?
- If you knew the precise date of your death, what would you do?

Sadness / Longing
- Of the things money can buy, what do you long for most?
- Talk about one big opportunity in your life you missed.
- What gaps are your mentors not filling in their counsel to you?
- Describe one major unmet goal in your life.
- What's on your "bucket list"?
- If you were to lose all of your money/possessions tomorrow, what would bother you most?
- At what age will you look in the mirror and no longer believe that you are young?
- Describe a time of acute, non-physical, pain in your life.
- When was the last time you cried? By yourself? With another person?
- Describe a time in your life when you have felt very lonely.
- Have you ever been stung by the betrayal of a close friend? How has the experience affected your other relationships?
- Whose death (someone close to you) would you find most disturbing?
- Where do you go and what do you do when your life becomes too much to bear… when you are overwhelmed… when you realize you are not in control?

- What has been your biggest disappointment or failure in your life?
- What are you carrying that need to let go of? What is blocking you?
- Peace lies not in external circumstances; peace resides in the heart. What is keeping you from being at peace?
- What are the most important elements of your life that deserve or need more time?
- What is an area of your life about which you are deeply troubled?
- If you were to die later today with no opportunity to communicate with anyone, what would you regret not having told someone? What is stopping you?

Life Mission
- Knowing what you know about who you are, what is the big thing you might be called to do in the world? And if you did that… what might be the BIGGER thing?
- How or when do you play small… or sell yourself short? Or, when do you tend to "go large" or pretend you are bigger or better than you really are?
- What do other people say you are exceptionally good at doing?
- Think of a time in your life when you were at your best. What was going on? What were you particularly proud of? Give yourself a name that exemplifies this time…
- If you could do anything, and if you had all the money you needed, what might you do?
- What might you set out to accomplish that you haven't had the time, circumstances, or resources to accomplish in the past?

Fear
- In general, I think people worry too much about _____.
- When was the last time you felt intimidated? What did you do?
- Who or what is pressuring you to make and spend money?
- Describe a time in your life when you were really afraid.
- If I knew I could not fail, I would _____.
- What was the highest risk decision you have made so far in your life? What made the risk so significant?
- Whose death (someone close to you) would you find most disturbing?
- Where do you go and what do you do when your life becomes too much to bear… when you are overwhelmed… when you realize you are not in control?
- What is your biggest fear about losing or leaving your current job?
- Think back on a conversation that did not go well. Prepare two columns on a sheet of paper; 1) what went on that you did not say? And 2) what was said? Talk about the "did not say" column. What blocked you from speaking these thoughts or ideas?
- Everyone is hiding something. What are you hiding? What is it that you don't want others to know about you?

- What are you currently struggling with that has you afraid? How do you think you might overcome your fear?
- When either you don't judge it is safe, or you want to isolate yourself from a group, what methods will you use (e.g., humor, sarcasm, criticism, pout, physically leave, go silent…)?
- What is your biggest fear about death? About life?
- What have you dreamed about doing for a long time? What prevents you from doing it?

Embarrassment / Guilt
- I have never quite gotten the hang of _____.
- What are a couple of things you remember (not so fondly) about your parents or grandparents?
- Describe a time in your life when you were very embarrassed.
- If you could change one thing about yourself, what would it be?
- One area I wish people would take me more seriously is _____.
- Are you (or do you want to be) more financially successful than your parents? How would you compare the quality of your personal life with that of your parents?
- What would be the most difficult news for you to accept about someone in your family?
- What, if anything, would you change about the way you were raised?
- If your life were "absolutely perfect", how would it look to you? How is your life most different from that now?
- Talk about a time when you were teased. What happened? How did you feel?
- What criticism will you try most to avoid?
- When have you made a promise you couldn't (or didn't) keep?
- In what area of your life would you like to have greater peace?
- What is your most trying temptation (e.g., power, money, fame)?
- What has been your biggest disappointment or failure in your life?
- Describe one very poor decision you have made. What caused you to make the decision? What consequences have you had to bear because of if? What decision would you make if you had to do it over?
- How have you made peace with your past? What is still hanging out there?
- What is the biggest problem or issue on your life today?

Life Vision
- Imagine that you are observing your own funeral. What will your loved ones say about the difference you made in their lives? In the world?
- What are the hurts that you carry from your past? Might be betrayals, lost love, shame, pain.

- What are you passionate about? What is the wrong that you feel compelled to right?
- What correlations do you see between your "pain" and your "passion?"
- If there were five things you could pass on to the next generation, what would they be?
- In the outdoors we teach everyone to leave their campsite cleaner than they found it. How will you leave the "campsite" (your family, community, world) cleaner than you found it?
- An emotion I feel, but don't usually express is _____.
- What are you feeling right now mentally, physically, spiritually, emotionally?
- I suspect that behind my back, people say I'm _____ because _____.
- Introduce yourself without words, using your body.
- If you were guaranteed honest responses to any three questions, whom would you question and what would you ask?

Any/all emotions

- Describe the last time you "lost it" emotionally (anger, grief, fear, sadness, or overwhelming joy)
- What secret desire do you have that you have shared with few people, if anyone?
- Describe a time when you felt you were totally out of control of the circumstances around you; when you couldn't think, talk, or buy your way out of a situation.
- If you could do one miracle, what would you do? Why?
- Using no more than three words, describe your spiritual life today.
- A sanctuary is defined as a safe place. Where is a sanctuary in your life?
- How do you define contentment or peace?
- Where do you find solitude or reflection time? Do you have enough?
- For you, what is the difference between "religion" and "spirituality?"
- How would someone else describe where you are in your spiritual walk?

ADDITIONAL RESOURCES

Many of the tools, exercises, and concepts are built on the work of thought leaders involved in the field of individual growth and team performance, including:

- Baker, Dan, PhD. *What Happy People Know: How the New Science of Happiness Can Change your Life for the Better.* 2003.

- Brown, Brene. *Rising Strong: How the Ability to Reset Transforms the way we Live, Love,, Parent and Lead.* 2017.

- Dethmer, Jim, Diana Chapman, Kaley Warner Klemp. *The 15 Commitments of Conscious Leadership: A New Paradigm for Sustainable Success.* 2014.

- Godin, Seth. *Linchpin: Are You Indispensible?.* 2010.

- Heath, Chip and Dan Heath. *Switch: How to Change Things when Change is Hard.* 2010.

- Hendricks, Gaye. *The Big Leap: Conquer Your Hidden Fear and Take Life to the Next Level.* 2010.

- Lencioni, Patrick. *The Advantage: Why Organizational Health Trumps Everything Else in Business.* 2012.

- Ludeman, Kate, and Eddie Erlandson, *Radical Change, Radical Results.* Chicago: Dearborn Trade Publishing, 2003.

- Klemp, Kaley. *Thirteen Guidelines for Effective Teams.* Agoura Hills, CA: www.kaleyklemp.com, 2010.

- Sinek, Simon. *Leaders Eat Last: Why Some Teams Pull Together and Others Don't.* New York: The Penguin Group, 2014.

- Warner, Jim. *Aspirations of Greatness: Mapping the Midlife Leader's Reconnection to Self and Soul.* New York: John Wiley & Sons, 2002.

- Warner, Jim and Kaley Klemp. *The Drama-Free Office: A guide to Healthy Collaboration with your Team, Coworkers, and Boss.* Austin, TX: Greenleaf Book Group Press, 2011.

ABOUT VINCE

My career has focused on creating memorable experiences and facilitating great conversations. I studied Recreation in school and believe all people are whole and do our best when connected in supportive community. Whether in the outdoors or the board room, my style is engaging, challenging, and fun. Others describe me as warm, loyal, and open. I connect well with those seeking personal growth, finding their "edge," or aligning with their core sense of purpose.

As an entrepreneurial leader in the social sector, I enjoyed bringing diverse people together to accomplish significant goals. I have been a successful CEO with hundreds of employees, and on the senior management team looking after 20 million members at 2,500 locations with $4 Billion in revenues. Authoring several leadership-oriented resource books has integrated into my work with executive forums and professional associations in North America, Europe, Australia, Africa, and the Middle East. My practice today is focused on guiding transformational change for individuals, couples, leadership teams, and forums.

I was married for twenty-five years and my two daughters are well-launched. After our divorce I came out gay and am now mostly single splitting time between homes in the California desert and the high country of Colorado. I love most outdoor sports, international travel, a stimulating conversation with a creative meal, and a nice glass of wine at sunset. More? Check out "The Good Question" at www.vincecorsaro.com.

THE PRINCIPALS FORUM

The **Principals' Forum** is a loose network of business, education, and social sector leaders united by a common desire for authentic relationships and vibrant community in their professional and personal lives. Effective forums understand the value of the outside perspective. Contact help@theprincipalsforum.org or 949-444-8292 when support is desired.

- Resources for Forum Practice
- Guest/Ongoing Moderation
- Moderator Training
- Forum Retreat Design and Facilitation
- Getting unstuck when Forum has gone flat
- Coaching and Retreats for members, executive teams, couples and families.